Titles

EDITED AND INTRODUCED BY MARY-ALICE WATERS

Soldier of the Cuban Revolution
BY LUIS ALFONSO ZAYAS (2011)

Capitalism and the Transformation of Africa
BY MARY-ALICE WATERS AND MARTÍN KOPPEL (2009)

The First and Second Declarations of Havana (2007)

Our History Is Still Being Written
BY ARMANDO CHOY, GUSTAVO CHUI, MOISÉS SÍO WONG (2005)

Aldabonazo
BY ARMANDO HART (2004)

Marianas in Combat
BY TETÉ PUEBLA (2003)

October 1962: The 'Missile' Crisis as Seen from Cuba
BY TOMÁS DIEZ ACOSTA (2002)

From the Escambray to the Congo
BY VÍCTOR DREKE (2002)

Playa Girón/Bay of Pigs
BY FIDEL CASTRO AND JOSÉ RAMÓN FERNÁNDEZ (2001)

Cuba and the Coming American Revolution
BY JACK BARNES (2001)

Fertile Ground: Che Guevara and Bolivia
BY RODOLFO SALDAÑA (2001)

Che Guevara Talks to Young People (2000)

Making History
INTERVIEWS WITH FOUR CUBAN GENERALS (1999)

Pombo: A Man of Che's *guerrilla*
BY HARRY VILLEGAS (1997)

At the Side of Che Guevara
BY HARRY VILLEGAS (1997)

Episodes of the Cuban Revolutionary War, 1956–58
BY ERNESTO CHE GUEVARA (1996)

Continued on next page

The Bolivian Diary of Ernesto Che Guevara (1994)

To Speak the Truth
BY FIDEL CASTRO AND ERNESTO CHE GUEVARA (1992)

How Far We Slaves Have Come!
BY NELSON MANDELA AND FIDEL CASTRO (1991)

U.S. Hands Off the Mideast!
BY FIDEL CASTRO AND RICARDO ALARCÓN (1990)

In Defense of Socialism
BY FIDEL CASTRO (1989)

Che Guevara: Economics and Politics in the Transition to Socialism
BY CARLOS TABLADA (1989)

SOLDIER OF THE CUBAN REVOLUTION

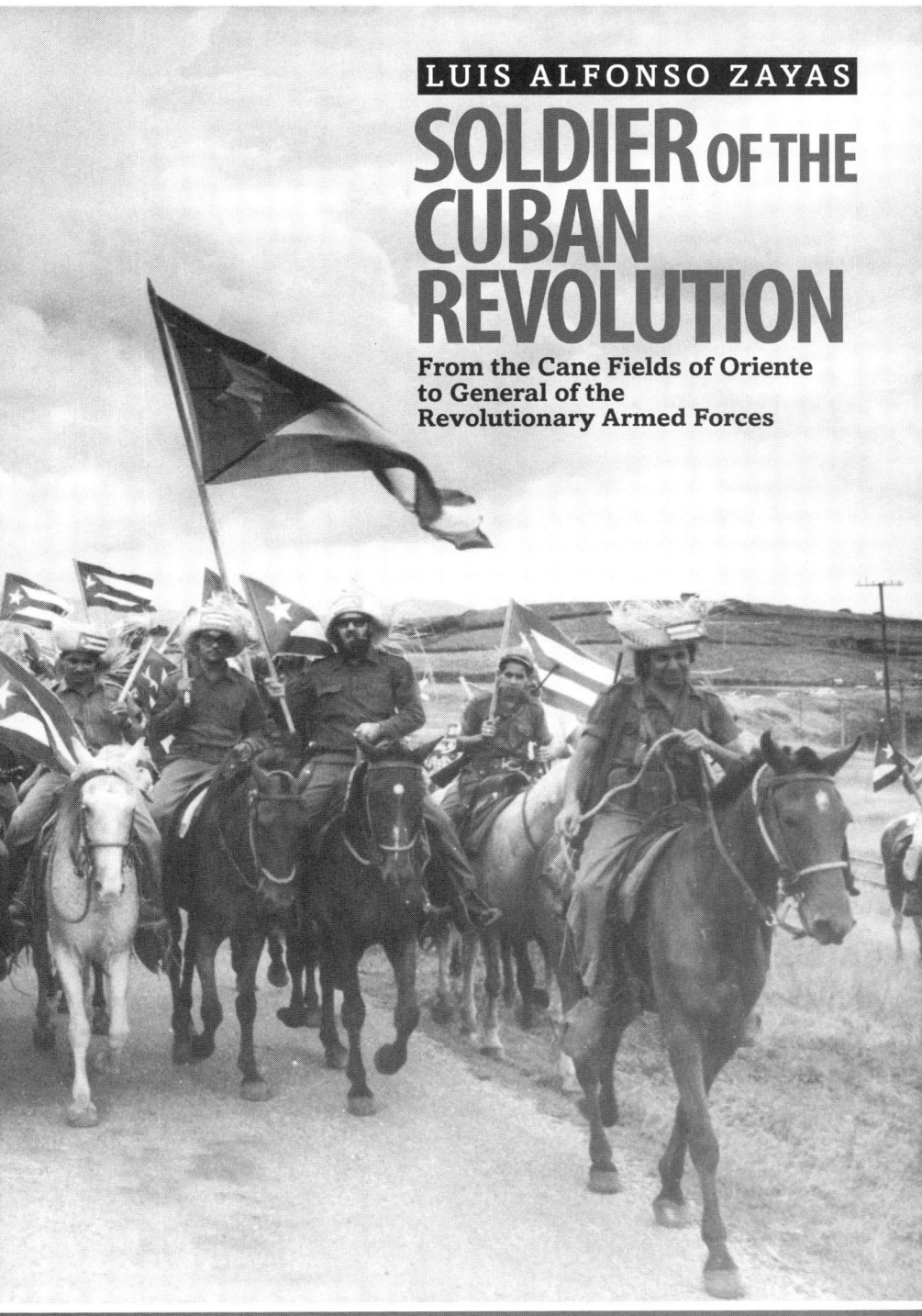

LUIS ALFONSO ZAYAS
SOLDIER OF THE CUBAN REVOLUTION
From the Cane Fields of Oriente to General of the Revolutionary Armed Forces

PATHFINDER NEW YORK LONDON MONTREAL SYDNEY

Edited by Mary-Alice Waters

Copyright © 2011 by Pathfinder Press
All rights reserved
ISBN 978-1-60488-031-1
Library of Congress Control Number 2010937307
Manufactured in the United States of America

First edition, 2011

COVER AND PHOTO PAGES DESIGN: Toni Gorton

COVER PHOTO: May 14, 1960: Militia unit of farmers, agricultural workers, and Rebel Army combatants, organized by National Institute of Agrarian Reform (INRA), rides to United Fruit Company headquarters in eastern Cuba to inform management of expropriation of company's holdings. (Raúl Corrales). Reproduced by permission. See pages 163–68.

Pathfinder
www.pathfinderpress.com
E-mail: pathfinder@pathfinderpress.com

Contents

Introduction
Mary-Alice Waters 9

Luis Alfonso Zayas 25

PART I
Cuba Before the Revolution 31

PART II
Fighting to Overthrow the Batista Dictatorship 53

PART III
Soldier of the Revolution 101

PART IV
Defending Angola's Sovereignty 129

Capturing a Moment in Revolutionary History: The Cover Photo
Mary-Alice Waters 163

Glossary of Individuals, Organizations, and Events 169

Index 191

PHOTOS
Photo section, following page 96
Luis Alfonso Zayas 24

Cutting cane, 1943	37
Home of sugar plantation administrator, 1920; family in front of home in countryside, 1950s	44
An Afternoon at Tinguaro, 1950s	48
Authentic Party election campaign rally, 1954	58
July 26 Movement in Puerto Padre, 1957	68
Rebel Army reinforcements with Fidel Castro, 1957	69
Battle of Santa Clara, 1958	94
Alfonso Zayas at revolutionary tribunal, 1959; with Fidel Castro, Juan Almeida, José Ramón Fernández, 1967	106
Mobilization for 10-million-ton sugar harvest, 1970	113
Alfonso Zayas in Angola, 1976	140

MAPS

Cuba before the revolution	22
Oriente Province, 1959	34
Sierra Maestra, 1956–58	72
Las Villas province, Escambray mountains	86
Angola	134

Introduction

MARY-ALICE WATERS

Soldier of the Cuban Revolution: From the Cane Fields of Oriente to General of the Revolutionary Armed Forces tells the story of the revolution in the most accurate and effective way it can be told—through the life of one of its protagonists. Luis Alfonso Zayas's story is at once both unique and typical of the young men and women, many still in their teens, who more than a half century ago threw themselves into uncompromising struggle to rid Cuba of a bloody military dictatorship, and dared to take on the propertied classes of Cuba and the United States whose interests that tyranny served.

Through Zayas's account, we come to understand how hundreds, then thousands, and eventually hundreds of thousands of ordinary working people transformed *themselves* as they gained confidence in their own collective strength "to storm the heavens," in Karl Marx's memorable words of tribute to the working men and women of the 1871 Paris Commune, the first government of the working class in history.

In refusing to betray the goals for which they fought, Cuba's workers and farmers accomplished what all the voices of both bourgeois authority and petty-bourgeois hesitancy, in Cuba and beyond, assured them was "impossible." They broke the armed might, and then the economic power, of the existing ruling classes and set out to create a truly just world order.

Mary-Alice Waters, president of Pathfinder Press, is the editor of *New International*, a magazine of Marxist politics and theory. She has edited more than twenty books of interviews, writings, and speeches of leaders of the Cuban Revolution.

They began to build Cuban society on a new, a proletarian, economic and social foundation, as they simultaneously extended the hand of solidarity to those in combat against imperialist domination and capitalist exploitation around the globe.

Soldier of the Cuban Revolution is not the first book published by Pathfinder Press that seeks to bring Cuba's socialist revolution to life in this way for new generations of working people and youth. It joins a growing arsenal of titles that includes *Our History Is Still Being Written* by Armando Choy, Gustavo Chui, and Moisés Sío Wong; *Aldabonazo* by Armando Hart; *Marianas in Combat* by Teté Puebla; *From the Escambray to the Congo* by Víctor Dreke; *Pombo: A Man of Che's 'guerrilla'* by Harry Villegas; *Cuba and the Coming American Revolution* by Jack Barnes; and *Episodes of the Cuban Revolutionary War* by Ernesto Che Guevara.

In each, the author tells the story of how as a rebel-minded young person they found themselves drawn to, and educated by, the revolutionary struggles of the Cuban workers and farmers who refused to accept the conditions of life imposed on them by the propertied families who owned the plantations, mills, and factories. And how they never turned back.

Several things stand out in the firsthand story of Alfonso Zayas as it unfolds through these pages.

One of the most powerful sections of the book is the author's account of economic and social relations that shaped struggles in the countryside as he was growing up in the 1940s and '50s, when Cuba was the largest sugar producer and exporter in the world and supplied 37 percent of the sugar consumed in the United States alone.

• The vast sugar plantations owned and managed by US capitalist giants such as the United Fruit Company (reinvented as Chiquita Brands International some years ago) and the Cuban-American Sugar Mills Company, with their comfortable

"American zone" schools, clinics, tennis courts, and swimming pools, reserved for the enjoyment of the resident US management personnel and a handful of Cuban overseers.
- The American owners' calculated policies to isolate their self-sufficient realms from the rest of Cuba, with their company stores supplied directly from the United States, roads that were little more than often-impassable dirt tracks, and narrow-gauge rail lines that connected to nothing beyond the boundaries of their plantations, some of which extended over hundreds of square miles.
- The precarious, often brutalized, existence of even those Cubans who held title to a few acres of land, such as Zayas's father, and were supposedly "free" to sell the cane they grew.
- How Washington's infamous "sugar quota"—the US-imposed trade "agreement" setting the yearly tonnage exported from Cuba to the United States—actually worked. How this quota was wielded like a whip against small agricultural producers, subordinating them to the giant capitalist enterprises and assuring that farmers not mill owners bore all the risks of cultivation.
- The desperate conditions in which the families of those lucky enough to find seasonal jobs as mill hands or farm laborers survived, especially during *el tiempo muerto*, the eight months of "dead time" between sugar harvests each year when there was no work to be had.
- The weight of this hundreds-of-thousands-strong reserve army of labor in the countryside, the existence of which was a precondition for the continued profitability of Cuba's inefficient sugar industry—and whose deep traditions of struggle reaching back through generations of resistance and combat against slavery, colonial rule, and imperialist domination were a precondition for the triumph of the revolution.

"Today's generation didn't live in the Cuba of old," Zayas

says. No one under fifty was even born yet when that Cuba disappeared forever. No one under sixty had even entered their teens. "They see photographs of what Cuba was like then, but they don't know how life was under capitalism.

"It's not that there are no problems in Cuba today," Zayas notes. But when young Cubans go abroad to offer their services in various countries, including Venezuela and Haiti, "they see the reality in these places firsthand, and that gives them a clearer understanding of what the revolution changed."

Soldier of the Cuban Revolution gives readers everywhere a clearer understanding of what Cuba's workers and farmers changed when they opened—and, to this day, successfully continue to defend—the socialist revolution in our hemisphere.

■

Through the account in these pages, we are able to participate alongside Zayas in the clandestine actions of the July 26 Movement in Puerto Padre, his hometown. We go with him and his compañeros in the initial group of reinforcements—the fifty-one *Marabuzaleros*, as they became known—who in March 1957 joined the twenty-two Rebel Army combatants who had regrouped in the Sierra Maestra mountains after their initial setbacks. Together with Zayas, we grow through the battles, both political and military, waged by the Rebel Army in its formative months. In the process, we come to appreciate in an entirely new way the decisive weight of the rural toilers who early on threw themselves into the revolutionary war and joined the ranks of the combatants.

The Rebel Army could not have survived without the years of prior work that made possible the supplies and lines of communication organized by the clandestine cadres of the July 26 Movement in the cities and the wide network of support not only among workers but reaching deep into the middle classes. But the reader can understand that without the broad support of campesinos and young workers in the countryside like Zayas—recruits used to hard work, accustomed to the rigors of rural life, steeped in the ways of survival, knowledgeable about the operations of Cuba's hated *Guardia Rural* and other repressive forces, and deeply committed to the struggle—the odds would have been poor that the few dozen combatants in the early period of the Rebel Army could have avoided annihilation by the well-armed military forces of the US-backed tyranny of General Fulgencio Batista.

Zayas himself underlines this fact in a firsthand description of the epic hardships faced by the one hundred forty men in Che Guevara's famous Column 8 who marched from the Sierra Maestra to the Escambray mountains of central Cuba in September and early October 1958—an operation expected to take forty-eight hours that lasted forty-seven days instead. "If we'd advanced by truck [as initially planned], maybe we would have fallen into an ambush and none of us would have made it," Zayas says. If we had covered those three hundred seventy miles "in forty-eight hours, perhaps we wouldn't have weeded out the quitters, those who didn't have the willpower to continue. Perhaps we would never have been able to measure the capacities of those who did."

■

That proletarian morality of the Rebel Army became the foundation of the Revolutionary Armed Forces of Cuba, the FAR, formed after Batista's military forces were defeated in battle and disintegrated by the power of the revolutionary mass insurrection that swept the country in the first hours of January 1959. It was the moral and political foundation of the forces of the Revolutionary National Militia, the Revolutionary National Police, Ministry of the Interior, and Cuba's internationalist volunteers throughout the Americas, Africa, and beyond.

The insight Zayas's account of the revolutionary war gives us goes far in explaining what the leaders of neither Washington nor of apartheid South Africa could comprehend. How was it possible for Cuba to mount the military operation it did some sixteen years later—not with a few thousands in elite units, but with a volunteer force that numbered nearly four hundred thousand Cubans over a decade and a half, volunteers who were willing to give their lives, as two thousand did, to defend the newly independent government of Angola against the forces of South Africa's white supremacist regime and its allies?

"Washington's great strategists couldn't even conceive of the kind of consciousness the Cubans demonstrated," the author says. And he is right. It is a class blindness they have never overcome, and never can.

Soldier of the Cuban Revolution includes Zayas's reflections on his three tours of duty in Angola between 1975 and 1987, serving at the request of the Angolan government in primarily civilian assignments. His story widens the scope of the firsthand accounts and documents available, especially in English, including those previously published by Pathfinder in books such as *How Far We Slaves Have Come* by Nelson Mandela and Fidel Castro, *Cuba's Internationalist Foreign Policy* by Fidel Castro, and *Our History Is Still Being Written*.

Of special interest are Zayas's observations about his work to help draw up development plans for oil-rich Cabinda province, which is separated from the rest of Angola by a strip of the Democratic Republic of the Congo (formerly Zaire). His account of the divisions within the governing Popular Movement for the Liberation of Angola (MPLA) and 1977 coup attempt against MPLA leader Agostinho Neto is similarly valuable, as is the description of the joint Angolan-Cuban military counteroffensive in early 1976 that pushed apartheid's reactionary, Zaire-based allies out of northern Angola.

What comes through Zayas's account is eloquently summarized in the words of then Minister of the FAR Raúl Castro, speaking to the final group of volunteers returning to Cuba some twenty years ago, in May 1991:

> If there's anything unique about the Cuban presence in Angola—which was the continuation of our best national traditions—it was the people's massive support for it. . . . Even more far-reaching and significant was the absolutely voluntary nature of the people's participation. Ours was not just a professional army, even if we take great pride in our troops' conduct in combat, in their technical preparedness—but an army of the masses, a revolutionary army of the people. . . .
>
> Faced with new and unexpected challenges, we will always be able to remember the epic of Angola with gratitude, because without Angola we would not be as strong as we are today.

∎

The "new and unexpected challenges" Cuba was already facing in 1991 were the consequence of the evaporation of 75 to 85 percent of Cuba's exports and imports, as the bureaucratic Stalinized regimes of Eastern Europe and the Soviet Union collapsed like a "meringue," to use the evocative phrase of then Cuban president Fidel Castro. There was an abrupt loss of vital supplies—from food, clothing, and fertilizers, to fuel, paper, machinery, and spare parts—losses that paralyzed every facet of agriculture, manufacturing, and transportation. Overnight a substantial, nearly thirty-year-long subsidy to the Cuban economy, in the form of favorable terms of trade and long-term loans, was wiped out. In response, Cuba's revolutionary leadership initiated what was known as the "Special Period in time of peace," and activated contingency plans developed to allow the Cuban people to survive even if the island were completely isolated by a naval blockade.

In the darkest moments of the Special Period, in 1993–94, Cuban families literally did not know from one day to another where their next meal would come from. But as Raúl foresaw, the hundreds of thousands of Cuban workers, farmers, and youth who had in the preceding years put their lives on the line in the struggle against apartheid South Africa *did* make the difference. They were stronger for that proletarian internationalism. They knew better the stakes they were fighting for and what Cuban working people were capable of achieving. Through the enormous efforts of Cuban workers and farmers and the measures taken by their government, production slowly began to recover. By the end of 1996, the very worst of the Special Period was behind them. And contrary to the predictions of all its enemies, the Cuban Revolution had proved in practice that its proletarian class foundations remained intact.

Throughout these harshest years of the Cuban Revolution, Zayas served as second in command of the Ejército Juvenil de Trabajo (EJT), the Youth Army of Labor, made up of special units of the Revolutionary Armed Forces that since 1973 have been a critical component of the rural labor force. Its units are organized, as Zayas says, to "fight, resist, and produce." Their contribution to meeting the food crisis of the Special Period was decisive, and remains so.

Agricultural products from farms operated by the Youth Army of Labor are brought into the cities and sold at EJT stands and food fairs for prices substantially lower than at other markets. This government policy implemented by the FAR assists those most in need, especially retirees scraping by on meager pensions. It helps hold down food prices by offering an alternative to farmers markets where prices are not capped. If an older person is short on money, Zayas notes, the established policy has been, "Give it to them. No charge." That's how EJT markets have been run.

A special period—with a small "s" and small "p"—still exists in Cuba, and will continue. The preferential trade policies, and other forms of subsidies and aid that cushioned Cuban working people against the capitalist world market, and against the incomparably greater productivity of labor in the imperialist countries, will not return. There will be no ceasefire in the fifty-year-old economic war waged against socialist Cuba by the imperialist colossus to the north. For the US ruling families, only surrender by the working people of Cuba would suffice; only reversal of the revolutionary actions that wrested fertile lands, factories, and natural resources out of the control of capital would meet their demands.

That is the goal Washington has been vainly striving to achieve for more than half a century. It is in face of this social and political fact that the battle to produce, the battle to raise living standards, the battle to defend Cuba's socialist course is being waged by the workers, farmers, and young people of Cuba today.

■

The *political* front of the US rulers' economic war has a different focus, however, and Zayas's account of the battles waged during the opening months of the revolution underscores this.

Conjuring forth, financing, promoting, and publicizing a "democratic" counterrevolution has been, from the very first days, the US rulers' political weapon of choice. The propaganda drumbeat never stops.

The goal: To persuade those around the world attracted to the liberating example of the Cuban Revolution that socialism, far from being the road to eradicating the myriad forms of tyranny and oppression produced by capital, instead means the suppression of individual freedom and inevitable narrowing of human rights—as has occurred in more than one country since early in the twentieth century and been defended in the name of "communism."

The imperialist campaign began in the very first weeks of 1959, as Batista's army of thugs were attempting to flee the country. Zayas was assigned by Ernesto Che Guevara to take charge of the prison at La Cabaña, the Rebel Army command post in the Spanish colonial fortress overlooking Havana Bay. "There weren't many prisoners at first," Zayas recounts, "but they quickly started to arrive." He continues:

> On January 1, in response to Fidel's call for a general strike and a popular insurrection, police stations and garrisons all across the country had been taken, and in the days that followed many of the regime's henchmen were captured. I'm talking about the ones who didn't escape with Batista—the ones who had to pay for their crimes. From all directions, at all hours of the day and night, patrol cars began to arrive at La Cabaña. In the end, more than a thousand of these thugs and murderers had been turned over.

As Zayas describes, revolutionary tribunals were established to hear evidence against each of them and hand down decisions. The outcry began immediately from the great defenders of bourgeois democracy, law, and order to the north. Cuba's popular revolutionary leadership was executing its enemies without due process, they charged. But the truth was the opposite. "No one was executed without having a trial with all established guarantees," Zayas notes. In fact, "had these individuals been released, they would have been lynched in the street. We had to protect them from the population. The people wanted justice for the deaths of their family members, their loved ones."

Responding to questions about these revolutionary tribunals put to him a few years ago by journalist Ignacio Ramonet, Fidel Castro explained further.

> Here, when [the dictator] Machado fell, in 1933, Machado's people were dragged through the streets; there were lynchings, houses were invaded and attacked, people sought vengeance, revenge. . . . So throughout the entire war, thinking about the mass violence that can accompany the victory of the people, we warned our country about that. . . .
>
> This may have been the only revolution in which the main war criminals were tried and brought to justice, the only revolution that didn't rob or steal, didn't drag people through the streets, didn't take revenge, didn't take justice into its own hands. . . . And if there were no lynchings, no bloodbaths it was because of our insistence and our promise: "War criminals will be brought to justice and punished."

One need only remember the corpse of Mussolini dangling by its feet in the streets of Milan, or the vengeful circus preceding the US-imposed regime's execution of Saddam Hussein in 2006, to recognize the powerful example set by the Cuban Revolution as it led the victims of Batista's tyranny to transform vengeance into revolutionary justice. Nothing throws the proletarian character of that revolution into sharper relief.

■

The interviews with Alfonso Zayas that eventually became *Soldier of the Cuban Revolution* were conducted by Martín Koppel and me in February and June 2007 and March 2009 in the national offices of the Association of Combatants of the Cuban Revolution (ACRC) in Havana, Cuba. Koppel is a staff writer for the *Militant* newsweekly and a Pathfinder editor. Another interview with Zayas, early this year, in which *El Militante* editor Róger Calero participated, added further details and clarifications.

The close interest and at times insistent inquiries of the executive vice president of the ACRC, General Harry Villegas—known throughout the world today as "Pombo"—were an ever-present stimulus. And the exacting work of Iraida Aguirrechu of Editora Política, the publishing house of the Central Committee of the Communist Party, was indispensable. She took part in every step of the process, from initial interviews to final review.

The famous photograph of the mounted militia unit riding toward the headquarters of the US-owned United Fruit Company in May 1960 to announce that the workers and farmers of Cuba had expropriated its vast plantations was given to Pathfinder more than a decade ago by Raúl Corrales, one of the finest photographers of the revolution. Corrales granted permission to reproduce that memorable photograph on a cover of our choosing, and no more appropriate choice can be imagined than this book.

Many of the other historic photos included here were supplied by the author. Others were located with the aid of the always helpful staffs responsible for the photographic archives of the periodicals *Granma* and *Bohemia*. And we are especially grateful for the help of Francisco Rodríguez Robles of the Youth Club in the nearby Jesús Menéndez municipality, who found, scanned, and sent us a photograph of the Chaparra sugar mill as it looked in the days before the revolution, when Zayas was growing up virtually in its shadow.

Above all, our thanks go to General Alfonso Zayas for his many long hours of work that made this book possible. The current and future generations of revolutionary-minded workers and farmers, and young people attracted to them, for whom this book is written, will now have a clearer view of the deep roots of the Cuban Revolution and the men and women whose actions made it the beacon it remains in the world today. They will know better the proletarian character traits and discipline they must emulate if they are to engage in similar deeds in every country the world over whose toilers are oppressed by capitalist exploitation.

November 2010

HAVANA
MATANZAS
HAVANA
MATANZAS
SANTA LUCIA
GUANIGUANICO
PINAR DEL RÍO
PINAR DEL RÍO
JAGÜEY GRANDE
SANTA CLARA
LAS VILLAS
CIENFUEGOS
PLAYA GIRÓN
ESCAMBRAY
TRINIDAD
Isle of Pines/Isle of Youth

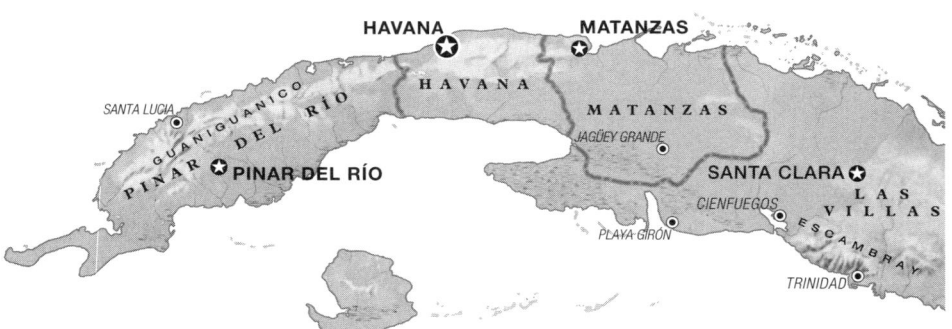

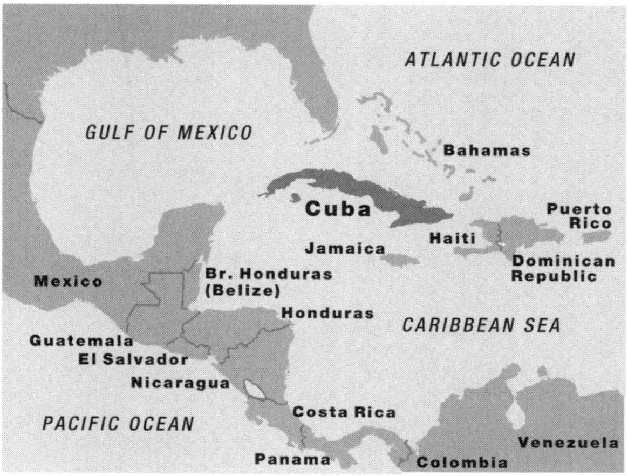
ATLANTIC OCEAN
GULF OF MEXICO
Bahamas
Cuba
Puerto Rico
Haiti
Jamaica
Dominican Republic
Mexico
Br. Honduras (Belize)
Honduras
CARIBBEAN SEA
Guatemala
El Salvador
Nicaragua
Costa Rica
PACIFIC OCEAN
Venezuela
Panama
Colombia

Cuba 1959

Alfonso Zayas (left) and Fidel Castro during three-day tour in Holguín province preparing 1970 campaign to produce ten million tons of sugar.

COURTESY ALFONSO ZAYAS

COURTESY ALFONSO ZAYAS

Zayas (center) with Ernesto Che Guevara (left) and Rogelio Acevedo (right), at 1964 reunion of those who had fought during revolutionary war in Rebel Army column led by Guevara.

Alfonso Zayas during interview June 2007.

MARTÍN KOPPEL/MILITANT

Luis Alfonso Zayas

LUIS ALFONSO ZAYAS OCHOA was born in 1936 in the municipality of Puerto Padre, in what is today Las Tunas province in eastern Cuba. His father was a sugarcane farmer. Zayas as a youth worked on his father's farm and cut cane on the Chaparra sugar plantation owned by the Cuban-American Sugar Mills Company. He attended school through fourth grade and then finished fifth and sixth grades in night classes.

While still in his teens, Zayas threw himself into the fight against the US-backed dictatorship of Fulgencio Batista, who had come to power through a military coup in 1952. Briefly a member of the Authentic Organization, in 1955 Zayas joined the newly formed July 26 Revolutionary Movement led by Fidel Castro, helping to organize a local unit of twenty members.

On November 29, 1956, Zayas led an attack by members of the July 26 Movement on the Cuban-American Sugar Mills Company's powder magazine in Puerto Padre, which was guarded by Batista's army. The attack was intended as a support action for the scheduled landing on Cuba's southeastern coast of the small boat, *Granma*. Eighty-two revolutionaries had sailed from exile in Mexico aboard the *Granma*—among them Fidel Castro, Raúl Castro, Ernesto Che Guevara, Juan Almeida, Camilo Cienfuegos, and Ramiro Valdés—to begin the revolutionary war against the dictatorship.

Forced to go underground following the attack on the explosives depot, in March 1957 Zayas joined the Rebel Army, then operating in the Sierra Maestra mountains. He was part of its first major reinforcement group. In May 1957 he fought at El Uvero, the first of twenty-seven major battles he participated in over the next nineteen months. When the second Rebel Army column was formed in July 1957—Column 4—under the command of Guevara, Zayas was assigned to that unit.

He took part in the historic seventy-four-day combat in the Sierra Maestra that resulted in the July 1958 defeat of the dictatorship's "final offensive" to crush the Rebel Army. Afterwards Zayas helped lead the Rebel Army's march to Las Villas province as a member of Column 8 under Guevara's command. Promoted to captain after reaching the Escambray mountains in central Cuba, Zayas participated in the Rebel Army offensive in December 1958. That campaign liberated the major cities and towns of Las Villas, culminating in the decisive defeat of the dictatorship's army in Santa Clara on January 1, 1959, and Batista's decision to flee Cuba the same day.

After helping to lead the column to Havana on January 3, Zayas was put in charge by Guevara of the La Cabaña prison, where hundreds of the Batista regime's torturers and murderers were tried for their crimes by revolutionary tribunals.

In 1965 Zayas was elected to the newly formed Central Committee of the Communist Party of Cuba, a responsibility he held until 1986. Promoted to the rank of commander, Zayas remained on active duty in Cuba's Revolutionary Armed Forces (FAR) until 1968, when he was given a civilian assignment as first secretary of the Communist Party in the Holguín region. He held that responsibility until 1972, when he was assigned to work as director of agricultural mechanization in Havana province. The following year he became deputy director of the agricultural department of the Central Committee of the Communist Party.

In December 1975 Zayas volunteered to join the Cuban armed forces' internationalist mission to Angola. There, serving on the northern front, he fought alongside the Popular Armed Forces for the Liberation of Angola (FAPLA) to defeat the US-backed invasion by the apartheid army of South Africa and its allies and thus preserve Angola's newly won independence. Zayas returned to Cuba in late 1976 following the defeat of the first South African invasion. He went back to Angola several months later to help organize Cuba's civilian collaboration with the new government there.

From 1978 to 1980 he was assigned to the Youth Army of Labor, EJT, the special unit of the FAR engaged primarily in agricultural labor.

In January 1980 he was named first secretary of the party in Las Tunas province, a responsibility he held until 1985.

Zayas volunteered for a third tour of duty in Angola from 1985 to 1987. He was assigned to Cabinda province to oversee the work of Cuba's internationalist collaborators helping to develop health care, education, communications, forestry, and other programs.

From 1987 to 1998 he was again assigned to the Youth Army of Labor, serving as second in command to Division General Rigoberto García.

Promoted to brigadier general of the FAR in 1996, Zayas retired from active duty in 1998. Since 2000 he has served as part of the national leadership of the Association of Combatants of the Cuban Revolution.

PART I

Cuba Before the Revolution

I. Cuba Before the Revolution

A colony of Spain for nearly four centuries, Cuba threw off the Spanish yoke in 1898 following more than thirty years of revolutionary struggles.

As Cuban independence fighters were gaining the upper hand in the last of three wars against the colonial regime, however, Washington entered the conflict. The rising imperialist power to Cuba's north quickly finished off the Spanish army and navy in what became known in the United States as the "Spanish-American War." US troops then proceeded to occupy Cuba as well as other Spanish-held territories—Puerto Rico, the Philippines, and Guam.

US rulers took the other former Spanish colonies as their direct possessions; in Cuba, however, they imposed a semicolonial system of domination. The "pseudorepublic," as it is known in Cuba, was enforced by a succession of pro-US regimes that ensured the country's capitalists and landlords fat rewards as junior partners of the Yankee empire.

By 1928, almost three-quarters of the country's sugar production was owned by US ruling-class families and the corporations they controlled. By 1958 about 90 percent of the island's mineral wealth and 80 percent of public utilities were in US hands. Oil refineries were controlled 100 percent by US and British corporations.

US-owned cattle and sugar plantations dominated vast expanses of land, some of them hundreds of square miles. A full 75 percent of all cultivated land was held by a small handful of Cuban and US owners.

Cuba's landlords and capitalists profited handsomely from this setup, enabling them to ape the social habits of their imperialist masters. Meanwhile, 700,000 rural Cubans owned no land at all, toiling as sharecroppers, tenant farmers, or squatters.

Cuba's main industry—sugar—employed half a million workers, most engaged in backbreaking labor as cane cutters or sugar mill laborers. But employment for most existed only during the four months of the sugar harvest. For the other eight months—known as the "dead time"—workers and their families made do with whatever odd jobs they could find, often going hungry. Some 600,000 workers across the island were totally unemployed. Out of Cuba's population of six million at the time of the 1959 revolution, close to a million were illiterate, with another million semiliterate. Over 600,000 children, primarily in the countryside, lacked schools. The average educational level for Cubans fifteen years or older was third grade.

Average life expectancy was below fifty-five years, with infant mortality over 60 per 1,000 live births. In all of rural Cuba there was just one public hospital and virtually no clinics. Thousands died each year of curable and largely preventable diseases such as malaria and tuberculosis.

In jobs, housing, services, and social life, racist discrimination against blacks and mulattos was institutionalized. Antiblack and anti-Chinese racism in Cuba had deep roots in the legacy of centuries of chattel slavery and indentured servitude. Under the US military occupation and pseudorepublic, however, segregationist practices modeled on Jim Crow in the US South were imported to many parts of Cuba. Whites-only beaches, clubs, and social events were only the most visible tip of the iceberg.

As for women, according to the 1953 census only 12 percent

of the workforce was female. Many worked as domestic servants. Thousands were forced into prostitution, servicing the wealthy US tourists who flocked to Havana's profitable casinos and sex shows operated by US-based organized crime syndicates under Fulgencio Batista's protection.

This was the Cuba in which young people of Alfonso Zayas's generation grew up.

MARY-ALICE WATERS: Most young people today, both in Cuba and elsewhere, don't know what Cuba was like before the revolution. They don't fully understand the naked brutality of the exploitation of workers and peasants, the extent of imperialist domination, the social conditions prevailing throughout the island but particularly in rural areas.

What was your life like as a young campesino growing up in eastern Cuba?

ALFONSO ZAYAS: I was born in the countryside in the township called Puerto Padre, in what used to be Oriente province. Now it's in Las Tunas. Sugar was the main crop. My father was a *colono*—he grew sugarcane on a small farm he owned.[1] I had four sisters, one older and three younger.

The two large mills in the area—Chaparra and Delicias—were among the biggest in Cuba.[2] Both belonged to the powerful US-owned Cuban-American Sugar Mills Company. Today this land and the mills on them belong to the revolution. Chaparra is now named after Jesús Menéndez, the central

1. See glossary, colono.
2. A sugar mill complex (*central*) in Cuba encompasses both the land where the sugarcane is grown and the mill where the cane is processed. In capitalist Cuba it also included the company-owned *batey*: the shacks where workers lived, the company store where they were obliged to purchase food and other necessities, and other facilities.

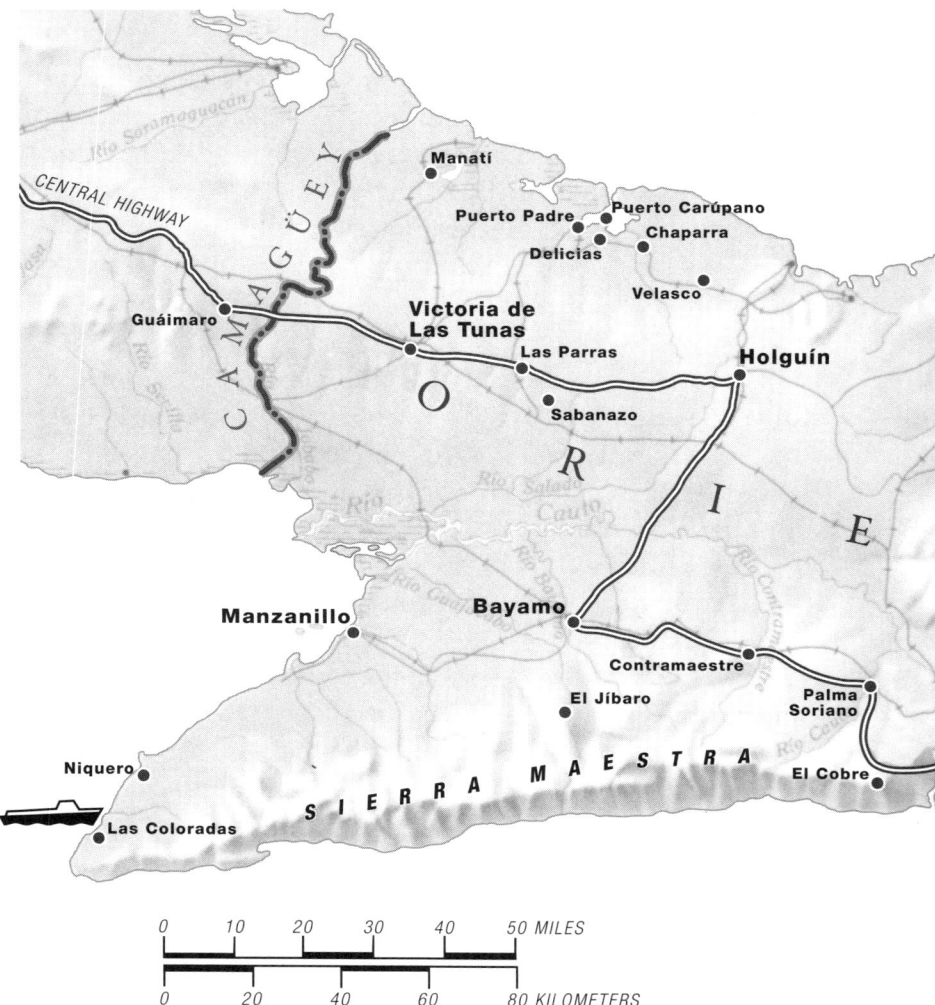

Oriente Province 1959

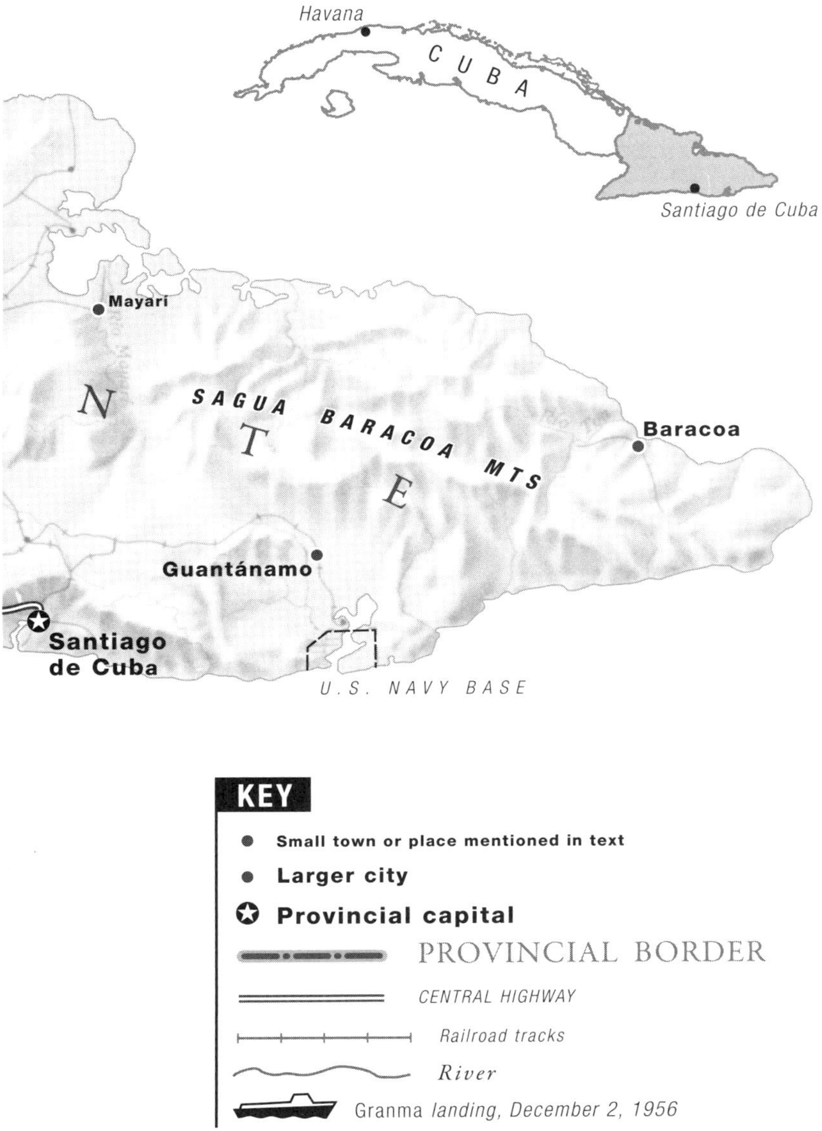

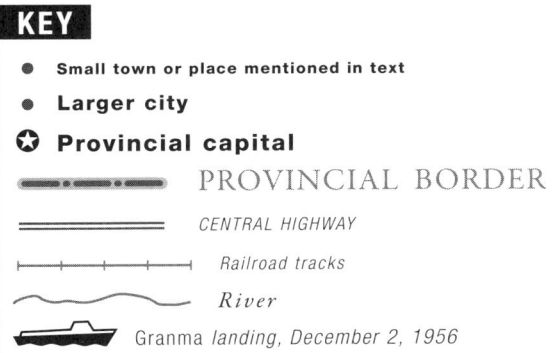

Havana
CUBA
Santiago de Cuba
Mayari
N
T
E
SAGUA BARACOA MTS
Baracoa
Guantánamo
Santiago de Cuba
U.S. NAVY BASE
KEY
Small town or place mentioned in text
Larger city
Provincial capital
PROVINCIAL BORDER
CENTRAL HIGHWAY
Railroad tracks
River
Granma landing, December 2, 1956

leader of the sugar workers in the 1930s and '40s. Delicias today bears the name Antonio Guiteras, leader of the revolutionary upsurge of 1933–34.

Since the 1959 revolution this land and these mills have at times been short of labor power. In those days, however, people lined up looking for work.

The sugar enterprises were huge. Thousands worked in the mills and throughout the plantation, doing everything from clearing the fields to working on the railroad. During the harvest, the mills worked three shifts, round the clock.

In addition, there were thousands of sugarcane farmers like my father. Everything was done by hand then, there wasn't any mechanization. That's why so many people were needed to do the work. You had to cut the cane by hand, lift it by hand, carry it by hand, load it by hand onto oxcarts. Some of the biggest colonos had tractors with wagons to carry the cane. The rest had to use oxen and wheeled wooden carts, like those you see in Westerns—carts made of wood, sitting on a metal axle.

The best-paying jobs in the area were in the sugar mill, where the wages were higher than for agricultural work. When I was a teenager, in fact, I tried to get a job there.

It wasn't so easy. You had to stand in line every day. If you did manage to get work, you were a reserve hand, that is, you only worked if the regular worker was absent. Then it would go in order: the first reserve hand, the second, the third, the fourth, the fifth—if none of them showed up, you could work.

We stood in line for the hardest, most difficult, most degrading jobs—hauling bagasse, a residue of the cane processing. You grabbed it with a hook and threw it onto the conveyor belt. The bagasse was burned to generate steam to power the mill. People lined up to try to be taken on as reserve hands to do that work.

AP

"Before the revolution there were tens of thousands of sugarcane farmers, like my father," Zayas says. "Everything was done by hand, from planting to cutting the cane to loading it onto ox carts."

Above, cutting cane, 1943.

What lengths did some people go to become reserve hands? They'd go to someone who had work and say, "I'll work in your place and give you the money." That is, he'd do the work and give the other person the wages. He'd work for no pay simply to have the right to be a reserve hand! Others who had no work at all sometimes worked in place of another cane cutter for half the normal wage, just to be able to work.

People bought jobs, too. There were reserve hands who paid one hundred fifty, two hundred pesos for a job, which was a lot of money.

When the sugar harvest was about to start, the bosses would use the trains or carts that transported the cane to round up workers. They took a train and went out picking up people milling around looking for work on the big plantations near Las Tunas, or Manatí, for example, which was the site of another sugar plantation.

Many of these men had families to support. Sometimes they looked for ten days, eating whatever they could find, since they had no money to buy food. They'd go back home penniless, since they didn't find work. And then start again.

WATERS: What about the "dead time," the eight months between harvests?

ZAYAS: That was worse. When dead time came, the only work was clearing the cane fields. There weren't many weeds, however, so there wasn't much work. And it was mostly done by workers who were regularly employed by the colonos.

It was really a difficult situation.

MARTÍN KOPPEL: Did the Cuban-American Sugar Mills Company dominate the entire region?

ZAYAS: Yes, nearby was the port of Cayo Juan Claro, now called Puerto Carúpano. From there the company exported sugar directly to the United States. They also imported all kinds of goods—groceries and everything else—that they

I. CUBA BEFORE THE REVOLUTION

sold. In addition to the money they made producing sugar, they made more through the stores they controlled. Almost everything, even farm implements, was sold through company stores.

Puerto Padre was isolated from the rest of the country. There was no highway, only dirt roads. They were impassable when it rained. And the local rail line didn't connect with the main line; it had narrow-gauge track. So to go to Las Tunas, for instance, you had to take the little company train that ran from the mill to where it met the main line. You had to change trains in Sabanazo or Las Parras to get to Las Tunas or Holguín. There was a little narrow-gauge trolley line from Velasco to Holguín. It ran only once a day, which was a nuisance. To get to Holguín you first had to go on horseback, or some other way, to catch that trolley. If you missed it, you had to wait for twenty-four hours.

The narrow-gauge rail line went to the various places where they loaded sugarcane—it covered three hundred kilometers. They used it to distribute goods to the stores in the countryside too.

There was also a dirt road connecting the company's two plantations. They stretched a chain across it as a toll barrier. Twenty-five centavos for cars, fifty centavos for trucks. It was a business, run by the company.

They had a whole brigade to maintain the dirt road. The brigade used shovels to fill potholes. They didn't even have a bulldozer in those days.

WATERS: The peasants who worked the sugarcane fields and brought in the harvest, where did most of them live?

ZAYAS: Wherever they could, as close to their jobs as possible. They lived out in the fields where they worked little plots of land. If they lived in the *batey*, the company settlement next to the mill, they were charged rent.

> Cuba's corrupt governments and the repeated Yankee interventions in the first few decades of the neocolonized republic handed over the country's wealth to foreign masters. The best farmland, the largest sugar mills, the mineral deposits, the basic industries, the railroads, the banks, the public services and foreign trade passed into the iron grip of US monopoly capital. . . .
>
> The economy grew deformed and absolutely dependent on US interests. Our country was turned into a supplier of sugar at low prices, a reliable reserve of supplies in the event of war, and yet another market for US surplus financial resources, and farm and industrial products. . . .
>
> Poverty, illiteracy, and disease were endemic throughout the country. The police brutally suppressed any expression of protest by workers, peasants, or students. . . . The whole apparatus of coercion—the administration, the parliament, and the judiciary—existed for the sole purpose of serving the Yankee monopolists, the landowners, and the bourgeoisie.
>
> FIDEL CASTRO
> DECEMBER 17, 1975[*]

WATERS: What about the small sugarcane farmers like your father, the colonos? What conditions did they face?

ZAYAS: The colonos were supposedly "owners" of the cane they harvested. I say *supposedly*, because the cane really belonged to the company.

---

[*] Fidel Castro, Report to First Congress of Communist Party of Cuba, in *First Congress of the Communist Party of Cuba* (Moscow: Progress Publishers, 1976), pp. 23–24.

I. CUBA BEFORE THE REVOLUTION

Between harvests, when they had no income, farmers bought everything on credit. The company gave you a voucher for ten, twenty, one hundred pesos, so you could buy things at the company store. But that was deducted from what the company would pay you during the next sugar harvest. So at the end of the harvest, instead of coming out ahead, sometimes you'd wind up in debt to the company.

Given the so-called quota system, practically everything ended up in the company's hands. Take my father, for example. Each year the company assigned him a quota. Thousands of arrobas of cane were left uncut, since he wasn't allowed to sell anything over the limit he was given.

KOPPEL: Why? How did this work?

ZAYAS: The company already had enough cane to produce the sugar it needed to fill its quota for sale outside the country. So it didn't buy my father's cane.

A field inspector from the company came by all the farms. He'd assign each colono a quota.[3] He'd set the figure at whatever he felt like. If you had a hundred thousand arrobas of cane, he might say, "You're going to cut only fifty thousand, you can't cut more." The remaining fifty thousand would be left for the next year.[4]

My father had four caballerías, which is about 56 hectares, or about 133 acres. He produced about 1,000 tons in each harvest, but they didn't let him cut more than 750. He was left with 250 tons uncut. He had two caballerías planted with

3. Each year Cuba was assigned a quota of sugar it could sell to the United States. The Cuban government then divided up this overall quota among the various US- and Cuban-owned companies. Companies in turn would allot cane quotas to farmers who supplied the mill.

4. 1 arroba = 25 pounds. One hundred thousand arrobas is 1,250 tons; 50,000 arrobas is 625 tons.

cane. The rest was pasture for cattle, or was used to grow fruit and vegetables.

KOPPEL: How was the inspection done?

ZAYAS: The inspector, who was Cuban, was one of the most important people working for the company. He traveled on horseback, making estimates of the number of arrobas each area would yield and assigning the quota that could be cut.

The company had a weigh station, as well as a loader that moved the cane from the carts onto the train's freight cars. They had a standard procedure. A cartload could weigh 7,000 pounds, for instance. But if it weighed 7,500 due to a mistake by the person loading the cane, then you'd have to unload 500 pounds by hand and leave it on the ground. Either it would get picked up later and put in another cart that wasn't full, or it just sat there and rotted.

And if you brought in cane that still had the cane straw, the leaves, you had to get rid of it. You had to strip the cane by hand of all leaves and roots. It had to be totally clean, pure cane. They set exacting standards, since they wanted cane that produced a high yield of sugar. Impurities reduced the yield.

WATERS: Were the US owners around? Were they involved in day-to-day operations?

ZAYAS: The Cuban-American Sugar Mills Company had its headquarters in the United States. The managers on the scene, the ones in charge, were Americans. There was Mr. Wood, Mr. Hicks, Mr. Shepard, Mr. England, and Mr. Williams. Mr. Wood was the top guy. He was in charge of both sugar complexes.

There was a residential area close to the mill where the managers lived. They had cars, which they drove on the unpaved road connecting the two mills. They'd go from one to the other in their cars, or on the trolley. We called it the

I. CUBA BEFORE THE REVOLUTION

buda; I don't know why.[5]

The managers also had horses that they rode out into the fields. One of them loved to hunt deer. So they had horses for hunting, too. They had hunting dogs, and a guide who'd take them where the deer were.

WATERS: Other than the inspectors, were any of the management personnel Cuban?

ZAYAS: In addition to the US managers, they had accountants and other specialists who were Americans. But the typists, the office personnel, the foremen in the mills, the person in charge of equipment, the superintendent of production, the chemists—these were Cubans.

KOPPEL: What was your family's economic situation?

ZAYAS: Like most colonos, our situation was difficult. I already mentioned the problem with the quota. But the colonos were also squeezed by debt. I'll give you an example I remember.

My father bought a little mare for me and my older sister to ride to school on. The school was about four kilometers away.

That little mare eventually matured and gave birth to a colt. My father sold the colt for ninety pesos. We planned to use the money to buy a bicycle. After I'd completed fourth grade, that was the only way I could physically get to school. But my father had taken out a loan, with interest of course. An interest payment came due, and he had to use the money from the pony to pay it. So the bicycle went down the drain.

"OK, dad, let's sell the mare and the saddle, so we can buy the bike," I said. He did sell them, for one hundred forty pesos. But along came another interest payment, and that was the end of the bike again.

---

5. The diesel engine of the light rail trolley car was manufactured by the Buda Engine Co. in Shreveport, Louisiana.

UNIVERSITY OF MARYLAND
AT COLLEGE PARK

BOHEMIA

During eight months of "dead time" between sugar harvests, when farmers and farm workers had no income, "they bought everything on credit," Zayas says. "You got a voucher to use at the company store. But what you bought was deducted from what the company owed you after the next harvest. So instead of coming out ahead, you'd often wind up in debt to the company."

Above, home of administrator at U.S.-owned Jatibonico sugar mill, Camagüey province, around 1920. Below, family assembled for photo outside home with roof and siding made from palm trees, a form of construction common in rural Cuba in the 1950s.

That's an example of what the colonos faced.

What did I do? I went to the fields where they were burning cane.[6] They needed people to cut the cane so it could be sent to the mill rapidly after burning, since it deteriorates fast. The colonos who needed to burn cane would let anyone cut it. I cut eleven cartloads, each one worth five pesos. And with that fifty-five pesos I bought the bicycle so I could go to night school.

WATERS: How far did you get in school?

ZAYAS: Up to that time, as I said, I'd completed fourth grade. Then, between night school and a private instructor, I reached the sixth grade.

WATERS: Was that typical of sugar farmers?

ZAYAS: No. My father, for example, never went to school. He learned to read and write from his parents.

My oldest sister left school after the fourth grade. After the revolution, some of my other sisters reached a higher level. But in those days, there was no school nearby.

KOPPEL: Did you cut cane on your father's farm?

ZAYAS: No, and I'll tell you why.

My father had four workers he'd hired. The small quota assigned him by the company allowed those four workers to eke out a living. But those workers didn't let me cut cane. Because letting the son of the owner do so would have reduced their share, since sharing five ways instead of four meant less for each of them. So they didn't let me cut cane. It would have taken food from their families' tables.

KOPPEL: What other jobs did you have when you were young?

ZAYAS: Various kinds. When I was a little older—by then I

---

6. Burning sugarcane before harvesting eliminates up to half the leaves. That results in fewer impurities being brought into the mill, reducing transportation and processing costs.

had joined the July 26 Revolutionary Movement—I got a job on the crew building the road from Puerto Padre to Las Tunas.

The crew the company hired to repair the road was headed by a Spaniard. He bought two dump trucks to carry rocks from the fields. It's not as if there was a quarry, with rock-crushing equipment. No! The rocks had to be broken by hand after being pulled out of the ground with pry bars, picks, and other hand tools. We'd use a big hammer to chip them into ten- or fifteen-inch pieces, which were used as the base of the roadway. Then we hammered the bigger chunks into two-inch pieces. They filled the spaces between the larger stones and became part of the macadam.

All the rock had to be loaded onto the truck by hand. The small crushed stones that became part of the macadam were loaded with a fork-like shovel, with each shovelful weighing over thirty pounds. You had to heave it almost two meters up onto the truck.

That was the job I got. Hauling rocks. At first I broke rocks by hand. But after a while, when I was a little older, I worked loading the truck. They paid you fifty centavos per cubic meter of broken stone you loaded. There were four of us for each truck, which held four cubic meters of stone. So each of us would earn fifty centavos per truckload. Some days we loaded four trucks, so we'd earn two pesos [the equivalent of $2.00 a day in the 1950s].

That was work for strong men. There were people who tried but couldn't do it. I've always been strong, so I could do the work.

KOPPEL: How did peasants organize to resist, to fight the conditions you've described?

ZAYAS: One fight was over something called the sugar differential. Let me explain what this was.

Not all sugarcane is of the same quality. Farmers would re-

I. CUBA BEFORE THE REVOLUTION

> To the task of liberating the nation from imperialist domination was inevitably added the task of eliminating the exploitation of man by man in our society. Both objectives were already an inseparable part of our historical process, because the capitalist system, which oppressed us as a nation from outside, oppressed and exploited us as working people at home. At the same time the one social force capable of emancipating the country from oppression within the country—the working people themselves—was the only force capable of supporting us against the imperialist power oppressing our country.
>
> FIDEL CASTRO
> DECEMBER 17, 1975*

ceive from the company a variable price on cane they delivered, based on an estimate of its yield of sugar after processing. But if the yield was substantially *more* than the estimate, farmers would demand the company pay them the difference, while workers demanded additional pay. Otherwise the company pocketed the whole thing.

That's what the struggle over the sugar differential was about. The sugar workers union played an important role in this fight. Today, however, this struggle is not well known or understood.

KOPPEL: In 1955 there was a strike of sugar workers in Cuba sparked by the fight around the differential. Did the strike reach Puerto Padre?

ZAYAS: Yes, a powerful strike took place throughout the

---

* Fidel Castro, Report to First Congress of Communist Party of Cuba, p. 26.

US employees at Cuban sugar mills lived in segregated quarters known as the *zona americana*. A traveler in 1929 described one such "American zone" as "luxurious bungalows, surrounded by trees, with spacious patios, often a tennis court and manicured lawns on wide streets…. In some houses there are even pools."

Above, *An Afternoon at Tinguaro* by Hipólito Caviedes. The easy life for owner Julio Lobo and friends at Tinguaro, one of the Cuban "Sugar King's" 14 mills, early 1950s.

I. CUBA BEFORE THE REVOLUTION   49

country, involving over 200,000 sugar workers. It was directed against US-owned companies, and against companies owned by Cuban capitalists like Julio Lobo.[7]

WATERS: What do you remember about the strikes in Puerto Padre?

ZAYAS: In Puerto Padre, whenever there was a strike involving sugar workers, what are today the Menéndez mill and the Guiteras mill would also go out. There was a combative workforce at both mills. The *Guardia Rural*, the rural police force, would step in and threaten the striking workers, of course. But since so many were on strike—everyone—they had to choose between the *plan de machete*, as we used to say—that is, beating workers with the flat side of the machete—or shooting them.

WATERS: What were other issues that gave rise to struggles by sugar workers and farmers?

ZAYAS: The sugar workers also fought mechanization because if you mechanized the harvest, you'd take away jobs. Under those conditions, the workers who cut cane would be left without work.

That's how it was in Cuba back then.

WATERS: Without knowing the conditions you've been describing, one has no sense of history, no sense of what the revolution changed.

ZAYAS: That's not only true for those under twenty. Anyone younger than fifty hadn't yet been born when the revolution triumphed.

They never experienced those prerevolutionary conditions, that capitalist reality.

---

7. See glossary, Julio Lobo.

PART II

Fighting to Overthrow the Batista Dictatorship

II. Fighting to Overthrow the Batista Dictatorship

On March 10, 1952, Fulgencio Batista, backed by the military high command, carried out a coup against the elected government of President Carlos Prío Socarrás. With the backing of Washington, Batista quickly established one of the bloodiest dictatorships yet seen in Latin America.

Many working people and rebel-minded youth wanted to take up arms against the Bastista regime. But the major bourgeois opposition groups and politicians were more afraid of an armed insurrection escaping their control than they were of Batista.

Among the young people determined to organize a fight against the police state was Fidel Castro. A member of the Orthodox Party—which under the leadership of Eduardo Chibás had won wide popular support campaigning against the corruption of the bourgeois regime overthrown by Batista—Castro initially sought to convince leaders of the *Ortodoxos*, as they were called, to put up something more than half-hearted opposition to the dictatorship. Having exhausted this effort, he and a handful of young workers and students set about creating a new revolutionary movement to do the job. By early 1953 they had organized some 1,200 supporters.

On July 26, 1953, 160 combatants, led by Fidel Castro, launched an insurrectionary attack on the Moncada army garrison in Santiago de Cuba, along with a simultaneous assault on the Carlos Manuel de Céspedes garrison in Bayamo. The attempt to seize the installations and confiscate the weapons inside failed. More than fifty young revolutionaries were massacred by Batista's forces, many after being brutally tortured. Fidel Castro and twenty-seven others, including Raúl Castro and Juan Almeida, were captured, tried, and sentenced to up to fifteen years in prison.

But the courage and determination of the rebels, as well as the regime's brutal response, moved thousands more Cubans into action. In face of a massive public campaign for amnesty, Batista's jailers released the revolutionaries on May 15, 1955.

In June 1955 the freed combatants, together with youth from the left wing of the Orthodox Party and other revolutionary groups, formed the July 26 Revolutionary Movement, its name marking the date of the assault on the Moncada and Bayamo barracks. The principal leaders were soon forced into exile, meeting up in Mexico, where they set about organizing, training, and arming themselves to return to Cuba.

In November 1956, eighty-two of these revolutionary combatants set out aboard the yacht *Granma* from Tuxpan, Mexico. They landed in southeast Cuba on December 2, 1956, marking the beginning of the Cuban revolutionary war based in the Sierra Maestra mountains and the birth of the Rebel Army. Among the expeditionaries were Fidel Castro, Raúl Castro, Juan Almeida, Ernesto Che Guevara, Camilo Cienfuegos, Ramiro Valdés, and others who would go on to become commanders in Cuba's revolutionary war.

The July 26 Movement in Oriente province, led by Frank País, organized a number of diversionary actions timed to coincide with the *Granma* landing. The most important was a November 30 uprising in Santiago de Cuba, the country's second-largest city. Another was a raid on a powder maga-

II. FIGHT TO OVERTHROW DICTATORSHIP

zine owned by the Cuban-American Sugar Mills Company in Puerto Padre. That action was led by Alfonso Zayas.

As Zayas relates below, he and other participants in these support actions subsequently constituted the first major group of reinforcements that reached the Rebel Army in the mountains in March 1957.

Despite initial setbacks, over the next year and a half of political work and combat the Rebel Army more and more became the catalyst for growing mass opposition to the dictatorship. Within towns and cities, cadres of the July 26 Movement organized effective support for the rebels in the Sierra Maestra, as well as actions to reinforce them and prepare the conditions for an eventual urban insurrection. The March 13 Revolutionary Directorate—born out of an action by revolutionary-minded students attempting to assassinate Batista—set up an armed front in the Escambray mountains of central Cuba in February 1958. Cadres of other anti-Batista organizations, such as the Popular Socialist Party (Cuba's pro-Moscow Communist Party, which had initially denounced the course of the July 26 Movement), began to be drawn into a united effort.

In mid-1958 in seventy-four days of combat the Rebel Army of some 300 combatants withstood and defeated what the dictatorship had dubbed its "final offensive" in the Sierra Maestra, carried out by a 10,000-strong force of the Batista army. The revolutionary army rapidly launched a counteroffensive, establishing three new fronts in Oriente province led by Raúl Castro, Juan Almeida, and Delio Gómez Ochoa. It also organized two columns to move west—one led by Che Guevara, the other by Camilo Cienfuegos—that soon established new fronts in central Cuba.

Zayas belonged to Guevara's column, which marched to the Escambray mountains in southern Las Villas province. Guevara was assigned to take leadership of July 26 Movement forces operating there, and to bring all other revolutionary organizations in the region under his command.

Guevara's column immediately launched coordinated operations in the Escambray with the guerrilla front of the March 13 Revolutionary Directorate led by Faure Chomón. In addition, smaller units organized by the Popular Socialist Party in Las Villas put themselves under the command of the columns led by Guevara and Cienfuegos.

Also in the Escambray was the so-called Second National Front of the Escambray. This organization, originally connected with the March 13 Revolutionary Directorate, refused to collaborate either with Guevara's Rebel Army column or Chomón's forces, carrying out no more than a semblance of a fight against Batista's troops. They came to be hated by the peasantry, from whom they seized food and supplies without compensation. Following the revolutionary overthrow of Batista, many of the Second Front leaders helped organize counterrevolutionary forces in the Escambray funded largely by Washington.

From October 1958 on, the rebel forces in Las Villas inflicted defeat after defeat on Batista's army. By late December, most towns and cities in the province had been liberated, and the Rebel Army was closing in on Santa Clara, the capital of Las Villas and fourth largest city in Cuba.

The battle of Santa Clara began on December 28, 1958. By New Year's Eve, Batista's forces there were on the verge of surrender, which would effectively cut the island in two. At the same time, the Rebel Army in Oriente was closing in on Santiago de Cuba. In the early morning hours of January 1, 1959, Batista and many of his closest collaborators fled the country, ceding power to a hastily named military junta.

From Santiago de Cuba, the revolutionary forces publicly refused to recognize Batista's handpicked replacement. Castro ordered the Rebel Army to immediately occupy Havana and San-

II. FIGHT TO OVERTHROW DICTATORSHIP

tiago de Cuba, and called for a revolutionary general strike across the island. Within twenty-four hours, the columns led by Camilo Cienfuegos and Che Guevara had occupied the main military garrisons in Havana. Batista's forces in Santiago had surrendered. A popular insurrection swept the country, taking police stations and military headquarters everywhere. The Rebel Army's main columns, commanded by Fidel Castro, rolled from Santiago de Cuba toward Havana. The Freedom Caravan, as it was called, arrived in the capital January 8.

KOPPEL: When did you join the revolutionary movement? How did you get involved?

ZAYAS: In 1955, around the time the July 26 Revolutionary Movement was formed. I was nineteen years old. At the time I was a peasant, with no political experience. I wasn't really a worker, since I had no regular job. I saw what was happening to young people and workers, and that there was no prospect for change. And I knew the atrocities the Batista government had committed.

WATERS: Were there other revolutionary groups in Puerto Padre at the time?

ZAYAS: Yes, the Authentic Organization, led by Carlos Prío Socarrás. Prío had been the president overthrown by Batista in the 1952 coup. After the coup Prío created the Authentic Organization, the OA, as the military wing of the Authentic Party.

The first person who talked to me about joining an OA cell was Alcibíades Bermúdez, a distant cousin. Alcibíades and Guillermo Domínguez—who later became action commander of the July 26 Movement in Puerto Padre—talked to me about the struggle. They told me about the attack on the Moncada garrison, what Fidel had done with the group at Moncada. That was when I joined the struggle against Batista.

PUERTOPADRE.NET

"Puerto Padre was isolated," says Zayas, "but it had a combative workforce." After 1952 Batista coup, Zayas first joined armed wing of Authentic Party, the main bourgeois opposition group. Disillusioned by opposition's refusal to fight—all words, no action—he soon organized a cell of the July 26 Movement, recently formed by a fusion of revolutionary groups under leadership of Fidel Castro and others who had participated in the 1953 assault on the Moncada garrison in Santiago de Cuba.

Above, Authentic Party campaign rally in Puerto Padre, 1954. That year the Batista regime staged elections as facade for dictatorship imposed in 1952 coup. Revolutionary forces called for a boycott. Authentic Party presidential candidate Ramón Grau San Martín withdrew just prior to elections.

WATERS: Did you have any firsthand experience with Batista's police, with the repression carried out in the area?

ZAYAS: I'll give you an example. Two local members of the Guardia Rural, a sergeant and a corporal, were known for their abusiveness, for their mistreatment of people, of workers. They were representative of Batista's army.

During New Year's festivities they took pigs, turkeys, and chickens from peasants without paying. They did the same thing to shopkeepers—just took things without paying. That caused a lot of resentment. It was one of the things that led me to take up arms against the government.

Fidel had organized the July 26 Movement shortly before this, after getting out of prison on the Isle of Pines—which we now call the Isle of Youth—in May 1955. He'd been sentenced to fifteen years for his role in organizing the Moncada attack two years earlier. But the amnesty campaign forced Batista to release him and all the others.

Alcibíades came over soon after that and told me, "Our cell's not with the Authentic Organization any more, now we're with the July 26 Movement."

That's when I organized a cell of the July 26 Movement in my neighborhood. It had twenty members.

WATERS: What kinds of actions did your cell carry out?

ZAYAS: At first we collected money, sold July 26 Movement bonds, and made July 26 armbands. We'd meet and talk about all aspects of the struggle against Batista. We were underground, very secretive, with our work totally compartmentalized.

Frank País, head of the July 26 Movement in Oriente province, knew of us through Guillermo Domínguez, who as I said was in charge of action and sabotage for the Movement there. Later on Guillermo went up with us to the Sierra, because by then his identity was known by the army. He was captured and killed a few weeks after we arrived.

The Cuban American Sugar Mills Company had a powder magazine in Puerto Padre where they stored explosives used for blasting at stone quarries to produce the lime they needed in sugar production.

This depot was near where I lived. It was guarded by a couple of soldiers, members of the Guardia Rural, plus two night watchmen. I was assigned to prepare conditions so that when we got the signal, we could attack the depot and seize the explosives for later use in sabotage actions. In other words, I carried out what might be called military intelligence work, although at the time I didn't have the slightest idea what such a thing was.

I started by making friends with the guards posted there. I told them I was going to be joining the army. I said I wanted to enlist and asked them to show me how to handle a rifle, so I'd know when I joined. Every two weeks they rotated the guard and two new ones came. When the replacements came, the old ones would introduce me, so I stayed in their confidence.

No one knew I was head of a group of the July 26 Movement infiltrating the army, not even Raúl and Orlando, the two *compañeros* who were to go with me on the raid. They found out two hours before.

On November 29, 1956, Guillermo sent for me, and we met at the sugar mill complex. Fidel and the other compañeros who'd been training in Mexico were on their way to Cuba, he told me. The *Granma* would be landing the next day. We were to attack the depot that very night, seize the explosives, and carry them off to use for sabotage actions, like blowing up bridges, all around northern Oriente and parts of Camagüey.

Other actions across Oriente were also planned. In Santiago de Cuba, Frank País was organizing an uprising on November 30 at dawn. Fidel later explained that his plan was for the actions in Oriente to take place after the *Granma* landed, not before. In those days, however, the communications system was poor. Frank decided to carry out the Santiago action in support of the landing, which, according to our calculations, was supposed to happen on November 30.

Had the landing in fact taken place November 30, the actions that day would have greatly aided it, since the uprising in Santiago would have distracted the army's forces there. But the *Granma*—which landed nearby, close to Manzanillo, by Niquero—was delayed. It didn't land until December 2. So the actions we carried out ended up hurting the landing instead of helping. They alerted Batista's army. As a result of the November 30 events, the army sent several battalions of troops to Oriente, along with artillery.

KOPPEL: What was the plan of attack?

ZAYAS: My house was right across from the depot, about a hundred meters from the entrance.

For our attack, I was given two revolvers in a bag—a .32 caliber and a .38 caliber, each with six bullets. After meeting with Guillermo, I rode off on my bicycle, with the bag hanging on the handlebars.

As I approached, the soldier on duty called out, "Hey, come here." He was about two hundred meters away, right on the road. "Just a minute," I said. "I have a physical necessity to take care of first."

I went to the outhouse briefly to collect my thoughts and calm down. Then I went to the guard and invited him over, saying, "Hey, we're going to have a little dinner here tonight." I went to the store and bought three pounds of rice, a can of tuna, spices, tomatoes, puree, and a bottle of rum.

The woman who lived next door to the depot agreed to make the tuna and rice. Her husband was actually a member of my cell, but he knew nothing about what was about to take place. We looked for a domino set, so we could get the guards to play. Then I went to get my two compañeros, Raúl Castro Mercader and Orlando Pupo Peña, to have them join me.

I talk about this calmly now, but back then I was just a young *guajiro*, a peasant. I have no idea how I figured out how to do all this. Keep in mind my level of education. People like me weren't expected to take this kind of initiative.

The plan was to take the two guards and the night watchman prisoner, without firing a shot. The night watchman had a pistol. The guards each had .45 revolvers and, when they stood guard, two Springfield rifles.

We were going to attack the depot at 10:00 p.m., since only one of the two sentries would be on duty then. One always went to eat at that time, bringing food back for the other. He'd be returning on a bus that came by at 10:20 p.m. The plan was to grab the guard on duty and night watchman at 10:00, take them prisoner, tie them up, and wait for the other one to return at 10:20. He'd come without realizing anything had happened. We'd grab him too, tie him up, and everything would happen all nice and peaceful. Orlando Pupo would be outside by the road, waiting for a car that compañeros in Delicias were sending so we could load the explosives from the depot and take them away.

That was the idea. But things didn't go as planned.

I'd given Raúl one of the revolvers, which he'd put under his jacket. We were playing dominoes, and the guards were drinking. I myself wasn't drinking, to keep my head clear. Raúl, who was very nervous, began to unzip his jacket. By about 9:40, he'd unzipped it so far down you could practically see the handle of his revolver. So there was nothing else for me to do but begin early. At 9:45 I jumped up, took out my revolver, and shouted, "Don't move! We're with Fidel Castro! We're from the July 26 Movement!"

You can imagine the scene. There was only a Coleman lantern for light. The guard playing dominoes with us had hung his revolver on one of the roof supports, which Orlando was standing next to. Orlando grabbed the revolver, but as he did so he struck the lantern and broke it, putting out the flame. We were left in the dark, and the guard took off running—with the key to the depot in his pocket. I fired at him but he got away. The night watchman took off, too, and turned up the next day hiding in a neighbor's latrine.

We headed for the shack where the rifles were kept. I grabbed one and Raúl grabbed the other, along with the cartridge belt. When people heard shots, the first to arrive on the scene was Raúl's family, who lived fifty meters from the depot. Then my family arrived and so did Raúl's uncles. There was a big commotion. Everyone was screaming, women and kids. My mother came over, so did other boys. "You're all drunk," some said.

"No, we're not drunk, we're with Fidel Castro!"

"You're crazy. What have you done?"

You didn't mess with Batista's army back then. Just seeing one of Batista's soldiers was enough to scare you.

"Let's go!" my mother said. "We've got to hide you under the bed."

"No, we're not hiding under the bed," I said. "This is war! We're with Fidel Castro! We want to bring down Batista!"

Then my father said: "Listen, you've got to get away from here. What you've done is against the law!"

So what happened?

The people in the car coming to pick us up turned around when they heard the shots. The rest of my group, the members of my cell, had been told to assemble near the sugar mill, by the local army headquarters. They were going to be given weapons to attack it. That order had been countermanded, however, and they were sent home. But I didn't know that.

It was clear we weren't going to get the dynamite, that the car wasn't coming for us, that the guard had taken off with the key, and that we were left with only two rifles and three revolvers—the two we already had, plus the one we'd taken from the guard. I decided to head over to where I thought the rest of my cell was going to be waiting, maybe six or eight kilometers away. We got to the spot . . . and no one was there.

So we were left holding the bag.

A cousin of Pupo's, who was part of my cell, lived about ten kilometers away. Pupo's grandfather had a small farm near the cousin's house. We decided to head to the farm in order to make contact with Pupo's cousin, so he could let the Movement's leadership know where we were. We arrived at his grandfather's farm at dawn.

Pupo went to see if he could talk to his cousin. While he was walking past a banana grove at his uncle's house, Pupo saw a couple of Guardia Rural soldiers with rifles watching it, to see if we'd try to go there. By dawn all our relatives' houses were being watched.

On the fourth day we managed to make contact with the Movement and were sent to a place previously agreed on. We stayed there for more than two months, until February 13.

Then, from Santiago, Frank País sent for us. The ones who came to get us were Guillermo Domínguez, who had gone to Santiago, and Armando García, a compañero from the Movement's leadership there. They moved us to Santiago de Cuba and later to Manzanillo, in preparation for us to join the first reinforcement group for the Rebel Army. That group was being formed outside Manzanillo, in a *marabuzal*—a marabú thicket—near a rice field.[1]

---

1. Marabú is a dense, thorny shrub that grows wild on uncultivated land in Cuba.

II. FIGHT TO OVERTHROW DICTATORSHIP

We had to leave the weapons behind and go to Santiago unarmed. We tried to disguise ourselves a little in order to throw the cops off the scent. We were on their wanted list. Our photos and personal information were everywhere, in all the army garrisons and police stations. If you had a mustache, you shaved it off. If you didn't, you grew one.

Since the Central Highway was the only route, we passed through Holguín, where the regiment was stationed, as well as Bayamo. We had to pass through El Cobre, where there was always a checkpoint.

The three of us traveled with a driver from Delicias who lived near the army headquarters, plus another compañero who was to accompany the driver on the way back. The driver was familiar with all the army's operations there, down to knowing individuals by name. When we got to the checkpoint, he got out of the car. A soldier came over.

"Where are you from?" he asked.

"Delicias."

"How's Lieutenant So-and-So?"

"Oh, he was transferred," the driver responded. "Now it's Lieutenant Such-and-Such."

"Ah, you're right. OK, go on ahead."

There were no problems. Even though we had no weapons, we had to be careful. In those days five young guys traveling together looked suspicious.

We got to Santiago; I still don't know how. They told us to wait in a park and someone would come get us. We got to the park . . . and no one was there. Around 5:00 p.m. Armando and Guillermo showed up and took us to a small hotel, the San Carlos.

We had just seven pesos between us. They left us there, saying they'd come back the next morning. Next morning—nothing. Noontime—nothing. Those seven pesos were all we had.

The hotel cost five. We couldn't eat lunch, since we wouldn't be able to pay for the room. The wait was horrible. Every time someone walked into the lobby and looked at us, we thought, "He's a Batista person. He's staring at us. We look suspicious."

At last they appeared, at 5:30 or 6:00 p.m. We were taken to a house at 261 Santo Tomás Street, a guest house they said was owned by Pedro Miret's mother. They left the three of us there. The place was constantly being fumigated—the "fumigators" were actually people from SIM, the Military Intelligence Service, looking for revolutionaries. Whenever someone from the family who owned the place heard the "fumigators" were coming, Orlando and Raúl would be sent off to two different houses. I stayed there, however, pretending to be part of a family. I lay in bed, claiming to be sick and have a fever.

We spent two weeks like that in Santiago, from February 13 to 27. Then they moved us to Manzanillo on the 27th or the 28th, to join the group forming up in the marabuzal. We became known as the *Marabuzaleros*.

Among the people working on this was Felipe Guerra Matos—Guerrita—a compañero who was very close to Celia Sánchez in Manzanillo. He was in contact with Fidel's guerrillas. Guerrita played a very important role in organizing the groups that went to the Sierra. He also brought the two journalists who went up to interview Fidel: Herbert Matthews went up first; Robert Taber went later.[2]

---

2. Herbert L. Matthews, a senior correspondent for the *New York Times*, interviewed Castro in the Sierra Maestra on February 17, 1957. The publication of the interview in the *Times* a week later had a big impact in Cuba and internationally, giving the lie to the Batista government's claim that Castro and the rebels had been annihilated.

Robert Taber was a freelance journalist. On April 23, 1957, he filmed an interview with Castro that was shown in the United

On March 1 we were taken from Manzanillo up to the marabuzal in a station wagon.

WATERS: How were the Marabuzaleros selected?

ZAYAS: All of us had been involved in support actions for the *Granma* landing: we in the north; those who'd been part of the November 30 uprising in Santiago; and others from Guantánamo, where there'd also been a support action, at the Ermita sugar mill. This latter group included three young Americans from the naval base who had been recruited.[3]

In other words, the Marabuzaleros consisted of those most committed to the armed struggle. We were underground and "burned," as we used to say. Our cover had been blown.

Frank País was the political organizer behind this whole plan. He was the one organizing things in Santiago, and he was very close to Celia and Guerrita in Manzanillo. Frank arranged for the arms we'd seized in Puerto Padre to be brought to Santiago. He himself then took the weapons from Santiago to the marabuzal in a truck loaded with oranges.

Those were the first rifles we got, and we used them for sentry duty: one guard in front of the marabuzal, the other in the rear. Since mine was one of the rifles being used by the sentries, I stayed by their side, sleeping right next to them. I said to myself, "If anything happens, that's my rifle and I'll grab it." More weapons came later. Frank kept bringing in arms.

We stayed there until March 15. Frank came to the marabuzal a number of times. Celia, Armando Hart, and several

---

States the following month on CBS-TV. Taber later became a founder of the Fair Play for Cuba Committee.

3. The three—Victor Buehlman, Chuck Ryan, and Michael Garvey—were part of the Marabuzaleros and spent several weeks with the Rebel Army. They soon returned to the United States, where they helped publicize the rebel cause.

COURTESY ALFONSO ZAYAS

"The first Rebel Army reinforcements came mostly from those who took part in the November 1956 actions in support of the *Granma* landing," Zayas explains. "There were fifty-one of us, more than double the number of the rebel forces in the Sierra Maestra."

Above, from left, Raúl Castro Mercader, Orlando Pupo, Zayas, and Guillermo Domínguez in Santiago de Cuba, February 1957, shortly before setting out for Sierra Maestra mountains. They were among the July 26 Movement members in Puerto Padre, eastern Cuba.

Below, Zayas, 1980, in front of old powder magazine of Cuban-American Sugar Mills Company in Puerto Padre. November 1956 attack on depot was carried out by Zayas together with Castro Mercader and Pupo.

COURTESY ALFONSO ZAYAS

COURTESY ALFONSO ZAYAS

New Rebel Army recruits meet with Fidel Castro (with glasses, right center) in the Sierra, March 1957. They include Raúl Castro Mercader (with helmet), Zayas (behind Castro Mercader, to left), Orlando Pupo (center), Alcibíades Bermúdez (just behind Fidel Castro), and Julio Pérez (bottom right).

Members of the July 26 Movement cell organized by Alfonso Zayas in Puerto Padre, Cuba, 1955–56

Luis Alfonso Zayas Ochoa
Armelio Acosta
Benito Bauza Benítez
Angel Bello Leyva
Argelio Bello Leyva
Giraldo Benítez González
Francisco Bermúdez Morales
Raúl Castro Mercader
Pastor Donne
Blas González Peña

Manuel González Peña
Luis Mercader
Félix Pérez
José Antonio Pérez
Leandro Pupo Peña
Orlando Pupo Peña
Dimas Ramírez
Edilberto Rodríguez Cazalí
Angel Soque Ramírez
Einer Zayas Bermúdez

other compañeros from the Movement's national leadership also came up. Not everybody, since too much coming and going would have attracted attention. But they kept in contact with us. They brought us clothes, uniforms, backpacks, weapons, ammunition, the things we were going to take to the combatants in the Sierra.

I was very curious about how things were going up there. When I was still in hiding in Puerto Padre, at the end of December or in early January 1957, Alcibíades Bermúdez and other Movement compañeros would bring us food from a house nearby. Whenever they came, I'd ask:

"Hey, what do you hear from the Sierra?"

"They say there are two thousand men up there already."

"Great!"

After they took us to Santiago, Vilma Espín was one of the people who came to measure us for uniforms—they came disguised as nurses. I asked her:

"Hey, how many people are there in the Sierra? Do you know?"

"Around a thousand," she said.

We eventually left the marabú thicket in two trucks, one of which was driven by Felipe Guerra Matos. They took us a short distance, but it was raining and the trucks got stuck in the first rice field we reached. So we had to continue on foot. We traveled that way all night. On March 16 we arrived at the farm of Epifanio Díaz, where Fidel had been interviewed by Herbert Matthews. Waiting for us there were Che Guevara and Ciro Frías, a peasant who had joined the guerrilla unit.

Che was there because he'd just had a bad asthma attack. Whenever that happened, he needed to take it easy for awhile. So among other things, Fidel assigned him to wait for us at the farm. The commander in chief was on the move a lot. Every day they'd march long distances, up and down the hills.

That night, after we'd met up with Che, we started the climb. We walked thirteen hours uphill, each of us carrying a load we weren't used to: a rifle, cartridge belt, backpack, sixty or seventy pounds. We walked from 6:00 p.m. until 7:00 the next morning.

We finally got to a place called Cayo Probado. By now we were up in the Sierra Maestra. I asked the head of the group that was leading us how many people were with Fidel in the Sierra.

"Oh, around five hundred," he replied.

On March 24 we finally reached Caracas Peak, the place where we met up with Fidel. That was a little more than a week after we'd left the farm. They put us in a clearing, an open area where we were able to greet those coming up the road. Still preoccupied with the number of people up there, I started counting. I got to seventeen.

"This must be the General Staff," I thought to myself.

I had learned how to cut hair from my brother-in-law, who was a barber. Back at the marabú thicket, I'd been given a comb and scissors in case anyone coming down from the Sierra needed a haircut. After we'd been at Caracas Peak an hour or two, taking it easy and chatting, they sent for me; Ciro Redondo and Ramiro Valdés wanted haircuts.

I had them sit on tree trunks so I could cut their hair nice and easy, and so we could talk. I wanted them to tell me how things were in the Sierra, and they wanted to know what the situation was like in the *Llano*, in the cities. I told them everything I knew.

Then I said, "OK, now it's my turn."

"What do you want to know?"

"Where are the other people?"

"What other people?"

"The rest of the troops."

Sierra Maestra 1956–58

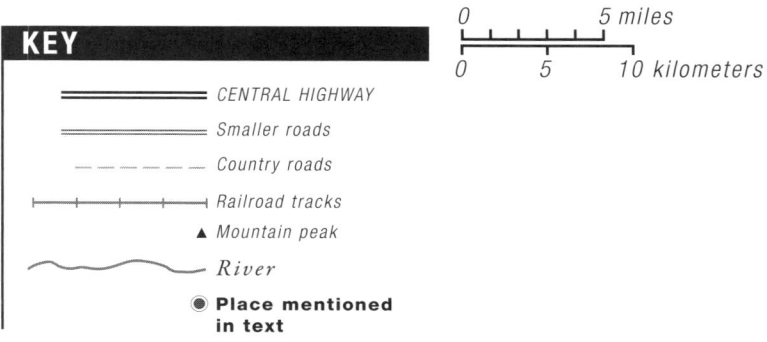

Manzanillo

Guacanayabo Gulf

Purial

Niquero

La Montería

El Lomón

Pilón

Alegría de Pío

Caribbean Sea

0   5 miles
0   5   10 kilometers

KEY

═══════ CENTRAL HIGHWAY
─────── Smaller roads
─ ─ ─ ─ Country roads
├──┼──┼──┤ Railroad tracks
▲ Mountain peak
〜〜〜 *River*
◉ **Place mentioned in text**

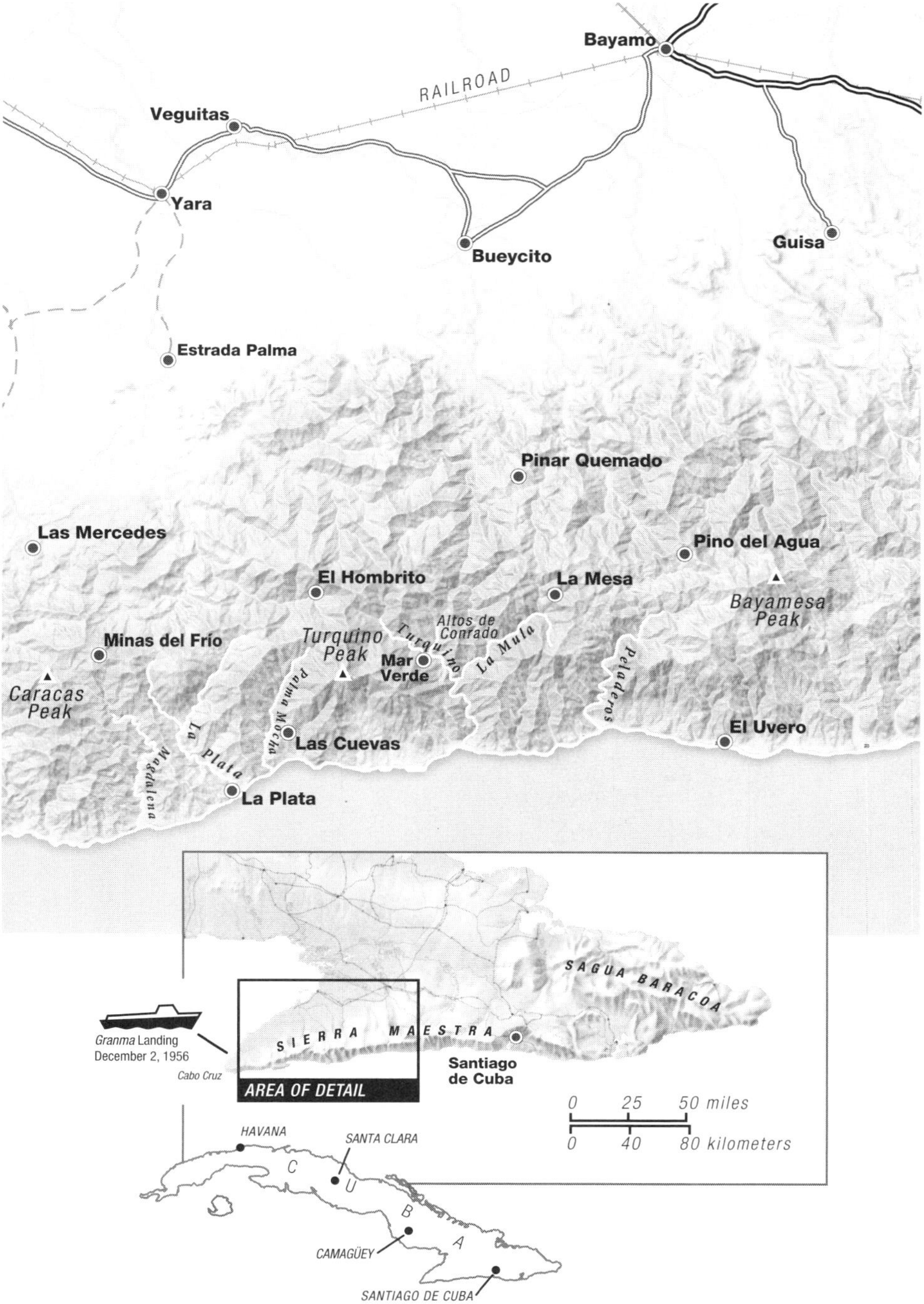
Bayamo
RAILROAD
Veguitas
Yara
Bueycito
Guisa
Estrada Palma
Pinar Quemado
Las Mercedes
Pino del Agua
El Hombrito
La Mesa
Bayamesa Peak
Altos de Conrado
Minas del Frío
Turquino Peak
Turquino
La Mula
Mar Verde
Caracas Peak
Peladeros
Palma Mocha
La Plata
El Uvero
Las Cuevas
Magdalena
La Plata
SAGUA BARACOA
Granma Landing December 2, 1956
SIERRA MAESTRA
Santiago de Cuba
Cabo Cruz
AREA OF DETAIL
0 25 50 miles
0 40 80 kilometers
HAVANA
SANTA CLARA
CUBA
CAMAGÜEY
SANTIAGO DE CUBA

"There is no one else."

"No one else? I thought this was the General Staff."

"Nope, there's no one else, chico."

Including Che, who'd gone to meet us; Guillermo García, who was waiting somewhere else; and Crescencio Pérez, who was away from the camp, there were twenty-two in all.

The two thousand . . . the thousand . . . the five hundred—had turned into twenty-two!

So the fifty-one Marabuzaleros were more than double the numbers already in the Sierra.

WATERS: Those fifty-one, how had they gotten to the marabú thicket? One by one?

ZAYAS: Yes, sometimes one would arrive, or little groups of two or three. The biggest was six. That group included René Ramos Latour, who died in combat later. He was to become the head of the July 26 Movement nationally after Frank País was killed in June.

WATERS: Was everybody armed at this time?

ZAYAS: Only one of us didn't have a gun; he had a knife. There's a funny story about him.

We were kidding around with him, saying he had to stay behind since he didn't have a gun. This compañero was a guajiro, a real Cuban peasant, and he exclaimed, "If you leave me behind, I'll shoot myself!"

"And what are you going to shoot yourself with?" we asked.

"With the knife!"

KOPPEL: What type of weapons did the combatants have?

ZAYAS: A few people had shotguns. Some had .22 caliber rifles. There was a Winchester .44. A number of us had Springfields. And there were two or three machine guns, including a Johnson and a Maxim with 30-cartridge belts.

KOPPEL: You carried ammunition for all those weapons?

II. FIGHT TO OVERTHROW DICTATORSHIP

> In spite of the serious setbacks the *Granma* expeditionaries suffered at the beginning of the guerrilla struggle, the first small group of fighters were sustained in those early days by Fidel's firmness and tenacity, which ingrained in them the idea of never giving up.
>
> The support of the peasants and agricultural workers was obtained first; the support of the working class and the rest of the Cuban people came later. All this constituted the great engine that toppled the tyranny. That came on January 1, 1959, when, with a firm base, we began to storm the heavens.
>
> RAÚL CASTRO
> JULY 1961[*]

ZAYAS: Yes. And we also brought ammunition for compañeros already in the Sierra. Plus we brought clothes, boots, and food—chocolate, powdered milk, condensed milk. And full uniforms. They were short on everything.

So when we got to the Sierra, people there were really happy. They needed help badly. The arrival of the Marabuzaleros was a big shot in the arm. It made possible the attack on the army's garrison at El Uvero two months later, on May 28, 1957.

El Uvero was the most important battle of that period. It was one of the bloodiest, with a tremendous display of courage from most of the compañeros who participated. Che said that battle marked the Rebel Army's coming of age, and he was right. The Batista government propaganda was saying

---

[*] Raúl Castro, "Eighth Anniversary of July 26," in *Raúl Castro: Selección de discursos y artículos* [Raul Castro: Selected speeches and articles], (Havana: Editora Política, 1988), p. 74.

at the time that the Rebel Army no longer existed, that Fidel was dead. El Uvero showed we existed and could fight.

We mounted a frontal assault on an entrenched position that included five strategically placed guard posts, each with three or four soldiers. The enemy was well-armed; all the soldiers had Garands or machine guns. We made do with whatever weapons we had, mostly bolt-action rifles plus a couple of machine guns. Che handled one of these, a Maxim. He was a doctor, the only one we had. But he fought as if he were just another soldier. And he was among the first to enter the command post at El Uvero when the soldiers surrendered.

Félix Pena had another machine gun. The one Che was using had come from Santiago a few days before the attack, smuggled along with other weapons inside drums of cooking oil. These had been brought up by the Babún timber company, which logged the forests in the Sierra. The shipment included at least one .30 caliber machine gun, the Maxim Che used, and a few M-1 rifles and Mausers.

The battle began at 4:30 a.m. and lasted about three hours. Fidel opened fire and, with his first shot, disabled the shortwave radio the soldiers used to communicate with Santiago de Cuba.

Batista's army had more than fifty soldiers at El Uvero. Their positions were reinforced by scattered logs.

Our forces by then numbered about eighty men. We were organized in four platoons—led by Raúl Castro, Juan Almeida, Jorge Sotús, and Crescencio Pérez—plus Fidel's command post platoon. Everyone took part in the battle, including those who had come on the *Granma* expedition: Fidel, Raúl, Che, Juan Almeida, Camilo Cienfuegos, Ramiro Valdés, Ciro Redondo, Julito Díaz, Efigenio Ameijeiras, Luis Crespo, Calixto García, Calixto Morales, Universo Sánchez, Pedro Sotto, among others.

Celia Sánchez was there, as well as those of us from the Marabuzalero reinforcement. So was Guillermo García and a group of peasants who'd joined up in the first days following the *Granma* landing.

In the battle the enemy suffered fourteen dead and nineteen wounded. On our side there were seven dead and eight wounded. That comes to a combined casualty rate for both sides of more than a third, the highest of any battle during the revolutionary war. In no other battle did we mount a frontal assault against such a position.

I fought as a simple soldier, a member of Juan Almeida's platoon. He was then a captain.

Almeida himself was wounded—three bullets in his leg and shoulder. He was at my side. I carried him on my shoulders. We set him down by a fallen tree trunk, where he was treated. Where I was positioned, we also had five wounded and one dead from the fierce gunfire.

WATERS: You said Che was both combatant and doctor?

ZAYAS: After El Uvero, Che stayed behind for more than a month to care for the wounded. In addition to those who recovered, Che's group also grew to include peasants who'd been recruited. By the time it rejoined Fidel's column, the unit had thirty or forty combatants.

By then another group of peasants had joined Fidel's column, along with individuals who had come up from the cities. So by July 1957 there were perhaps one hundred eighty combatants in all. That's when Fidel decided to divide the forces into two columns and named Che commander of the second one.

I asked to be in Che's column. I liked how Che acted, his sense of justice. But the main thing was to avoid the long marches Fidel was accustomed to making every day, something that certainly wasn't a custom for me.

The first battle I took part in as a member of Che's column was the capture of the garrison at Bueycito, a town on the plains, near Bayamo. We caught the army by surprise while they were sleeping, and they surrendered. We suffered one dead, and the army had a few wounded. We got something like sixteen rifles from the garrison. It was the column's first victory in battle.

Later I took part in the battle of El Hombrito, in a valley near a place called Pinar Quemado. Following that battle, Che promoted me to lieutenant.

At the site of that battle, Che set up a camp for new recruits and established a bakery, a shoe repair shop, a workshop to make uniforms, and vegetable gardens for growing food. Nearby, in Altos de Conrado, Radio Rebelde was set up.

WATERS: A workshop to make munitions as well?

ZAYAS: Yes. We had a little factory that made "M-26" rockets—or "Sputniks," as we called them. We made them from tin cans and explosives. The M-26 had a fuse that you lit. You put it on the end of a shotgun, fired the shotgun, and the M-26 would explode on impact when it landed—like a mortar. It didn't produce much shrapnel, but it had its uses. More than anything, it made a lot of noise.

WATERS: Can you talk about the work you did to gain the confidence of the peasants in the Sierra?

ZAYAS: In the area around El Hombrito, as elsewhere, Che played an important role in this. He'd meet and talk with the peasants. He'd get them together to explain the objectives of the revolution, to explain that there was going to be an agrarian reform to give land to the peasants.

As a doctor, Che also provided medical attention to the rural population, to the peasants. He called himself the "toothpuller" since, along with everything else, he used to act as dentist to Rebel Army soldiers and peasants alike.

One day I had a bad toothache. I went looking for Che so he could extract my tooth and get rid of the pain.

"He's over in that *bohío*, pulling teeth," someone said.

I headed to the thatched hut, and as I was arriving I heard a woman screaming.

"What's wrong?" I asked. "Why is she screaming like that?"

"Because there's no anesthesia."

My toothache disappeared on the spot. The pain had been scared out of me. I left without getting my tooth pulled.

Everyplace Che went, he would get the peasants together, or workers from the rice fields, and explain the struggle that had to be carried out to solve their problems.

Che did this throughout the entire war, in the Sierra Maestra, during the invasion—the march to Las Villas—and afterward in the Escambray mountains. He thought it was important to explain to the peasants what the revolution was, the objectives of the struggle, and what they had to do to fight the landlords, the bosses, and the government. Che was good at getting Fidel's message across.

KOPPEL: How did the Batista army respond to the support you were winning from the peasants?

ZAYAS: With brutality.

Among those pursuing us in the Sierra Maestra was a Batista army officer named Ángel Sánchez Mosquera. He moved around the Sierra burning down peasant homes. As the army approached, the peasants would flee their houses. When the soldiers showed up, they took everything they could—the animals, anything of value. Then they burned the houses. There were instances where they burned houses with peasants inside, accusing them of collaborating with us against Batista's army.

One time Sánchez Mosquera's company was going through

the Sierra, and we—Che's column—were in the area near Mar Verde. We were able to follow them simply by watching for smoke from houses they were burning.

At the time, Camilo Cienfuegos was in charge of the forward detachment of Che's column. Che had Camilo circle around and take up a position ahead of Sánchez Mosquera's troops, to try to catch them in a crossfire. But they fought very hard, and Camilo couldn't hold them back. Our forces inflicted four casualties on them but had to retreat.

Sánchez Mosquera's company withdrew to Mar Verde, a settlement, not quite a village. They had only a few soldiers, perhaps seventy. Three of them were advancing ahead of the rest, and we surrounded and captured them. They had very good weapons, three Garands. But a battalion of some four hundred soldiers came up from the coast as reinforcements, and we had no chance of resisting that kind of force. One squad did ambush them, but with one squad up against four hundred troops, we had to retreat.

Ciro Redondo was killed in the battle of Mar Verde. Ciro was exchanging fire with one soldier when another one got a shot at him from an angle and killed him. Later, during the invasion, Column 8 took the name "Ciro Redondo."

Ciro was a *Granma* expeditionary who had also taken part in the assault on the Moncada. He was a great compañero and an energetic combatant, very brave. He had a military bearing. Even under the conditions in the Sierra, he was always very clean and well dressed. We were together from the day I gave him a haircut after I arrived in the Sierra, up until he was killed in Mar Verde.

Ciro's death was a great loss. He, Ramiro Valdés, and Julio Díaz—who died at El Uvero—were very close friends from Artemisa. They were always together. They even resembled each other—in their physiques, in how they carried themselves. In addition to the loss of Ciro, a number of Rebel fighters were wounded, including Joel Iglesias. The prisoners we captured were the ones who had shot Joel.

Sánchez Mosquera's soldiers, plus the reinforcements who came from the coast, then advanced toward El Hombrito and took the entire area. We had to retreat from there.

Che ordered us to dismantle everything we'd built—the bakery, everything. He sent it all to La Mesa, which was a very out-of-the-way place. A peasant there named Polo Torres had put his plot of land at the disposal of the revolution, of the Rebel Army. He was known as "Capitán Descalzo" [Captain Barefoot], since he never wore shoes, and still doesn't. He lives on a farm near Manzanillo.

After we moved everything to La Mesa, the column split up, divided into platoons. Fidel sent Che to Minas del Frío to train the new recruits, and Ramiro was named head of Column 4. The school at Minas del Frío was for general education and basic training. We were creating conditions to sustain a long struggle if necessary.

In late May 1958 the Batista army started its big offensive in the Sierra Maestra to annihilate the rebels.[4] I was in charge of a platoon in the area of Las Mercedes, serving under Che's orders. Even though Ramiro had replaced Che as head of Column 4, Che, from his base in Minas del Frío, was actually leading us in the Las Mercedes area.

4. In late May 1958 the Batista army launched an "encircle and annihilate" offensive in the Sierra Maestra. The Rebel Army concentrated its forces to confront the troops of the dictatorship. By the time the army's offensive had been defeated in July 1958, the Rebel Army had inflicted more than one thousand casualties on Batista's forces, had grown to eight hundred combatants, and had captured six hundred weapons. Building on the momentum of this victory, the Rebel Army counterattacked and went on an offensive.

The Batista army's great offensive ended in defeat. The Rebel Army was strengthened, capturing plenty of weapons, good ones, and lots of ammunition. This made it possible to create the two columns that carried out the invasion, moving from Oriente to Las Villas: Column 8 commanded by Che, and Column 2 commanded by Camilo.[5] One of our objectives was to prevent army forces moving from Havana to Oriente.

WATERS: Why did Fidel select Che and Camilo to lead the two columns?

ZAYAS: Because they had demonstrated their audacity, their intelligence, their ability to lead others—from the training in Mexico, to the *Granma* landing here in Cuba and afterward, through the battles of La Plata, Arroyo del Infierno, Palma Mocha, El Uvero, and countering the offensive by the Batista army.[6]

At the end of March, Fidel sent Camilo to fight in the Holguín-Las Tunas-Bayamo area and to assess the possibilities for carrying the struggle into the Llano. Camilo and his platoon showed it could be done. He'd been encircled by the Batista army and had broken out.

When the army's big offensive came, Fidel ordered Camilo to return to the Sierra, where he fought several battles against powerful enemy forces. While fighting in the Sierra he cre-

5. The column led by Camilo Cienfuegos had originally been given the task of crossing the entire length of the island to establish a front in the mountains of Pinar del Río in western Cuba. In October, however, Fidel Castro ordered Cienfuegos to stay in northern Las Villas province until his troops could physically regain their strength and the next stage of the campaign could be adequately prepared.

6. Explanations and descriptions of all these events and battles can be found in Ernesto Che Guevara, *Episodes of the Cuban Revolutionary War 1956–58* (Pathfinder, 1996).

II. FIGHT TO OVERTHROW DICTATORSHIP

> Batista's army came out of that last offensive in the Sierra Maestra with its spine broken, but it had not yet been defeated. The struggle would go on. It was then that the final strategy was established, attacking along three points: Santiago de Cuba, which was put under a flexible siege; Las Villas, where I was to go; and Pinar del Río, at the other end of the island, where Camilo Cienfuegos, who was now commander of the "Antonio Maceo" Column no. 2, was to march in remembrance of the historic invasion by the great leader of 1895, when Maceo crossed the length of Cuban territory with epic feats, culminating in Mantua. Camilo Cienfuegos was not able to fulfill the second part of his program, as the exigencies of the war forced him to remain in Las Villas. . . .
>
> My orders were that the main strategic task was to systematically cut off communications between the two ends of the island. I was also ordered to establish relations with all the political groups that might be in the mountains of that region, and I was given broad powers to militarily govern my assigned area.
>
> ERNESTO CHE GUEVARA
> JUNE 16, 1959*

ated a strong column, well-armed, the one that later carried out the invasion.

Che had already proven himself as head of a column. Remember, Che was the first commander named by Fidel, the

---

* Ernesto Che Guevara, "From Batista's Final Offensive to the Battle of Santa Clara," in *Episodes of the Cuban Revolutionary War 1956–58*, pp. 357–58 [2010 printing].

first to be made head of a column. Like Raúl and Almeida, who became heads of the Second and Third Fronts, Che had shown his capacity, his courage, his leadership qualities. These three compañeros stood out.

From the time of the *Granma* landing, Che and Camilo were close. The only person who could play tricks on Che, for example, was Camilo. And Che would smile at these practical jokes. Camilo was a typical Cuban, a prankster, always joking, happy-go-lucky. Che was different. He was stern, very reserved. He inspired respect. Che was an Argentine. But Camilo used to horse around with Che as if he were Cuban.

KOPPEL: You were part of Che's Column 8, weren't you—the invasion, as it is known, that crossed Cuba from the Sierras?

ZAYAS: Yes, we left the Sierra Maestra from a place called Jíbaro on August 31. The march to Las Villas took forty-seven days. Che's column had one hundred forty men and Camilo's had around ninety. We marched on foot a little more than six hundred kilometers, in terrible conditions. It was in September and October, hurricane season, and we got hit by two of them—some say three. We marched along the coast the entire time, which meant we had to put up with water, mud, mosquitoes, and little or no food.

We went four days without eating once. We had no fresh food with us at all. We did have rice, beans, and other things. All this had to be cooked, however, and we couldn't cook since the army was dug in by the railroad tracks. They would have spotted our fires. So we marched three days without eating.

On the fourth day we got to a wooded area, where there was a peasant who raised pigs. Che bought two of those big pigs. As we were getting ready to cook them at dawn, an enemy aircraft appeared. An informer had reported us, so we had to abandon it all. The last plane circling and strafing us left at around 9:00 p.m. We went back looking for the pigs we'd been preparing, but we couldn't find them in the dark. We had to go into the lagoon, with water up to our waists, walking more or less like that through the night. The whole next day was really tough. That made four days without food.

Around midnight we came to a small settlement, with a cattle shed. We were given a little guava paste with cheese.

With the fifth day dawning, we finally ate a meal, which Che had ordered be prepared for us. We slaughtered a cow and ate it with rice and beans, as well as boiled plantains. That was about 2:30 a.m.

While we were at the dairy farm, we got hit by a second hurricane. It was like an ocean. The water was knee-high everywhere, since Camagüey is flat and we were along the coast. While the hurricane was still passing over, however, we ended up having to get out of there. The reason was that although our presence was supposed to be a secret, a compañero on guard duty had given twenty-five centavos to a young boy to buy honey for him at a grocery store. Meanwhile, Che had sent a contact to buy us food at the same store. While our contact was there, the boy came in.

"Give me twenty-five centavos worth of honey for the rebels over at the dairy farm," he said.

We had to take immediate measures, since army troops were nearby. The compañero who sent for the honey was put under arrest, and we went on alert. With rain from the hurricane still coming down, we had to move to a wooded area nearby, into knee-deep water—all due to the indiscipline of the person on guard duty. If the army came, Che said, we'd have to shoot the guard. He's lucky they didn't come and he's still alive.

We crossed the Júcaro-Morón line, which runs from south to north between these two towns and was controlled by the army. It was built during the independence wars against

Las Villas province 1958

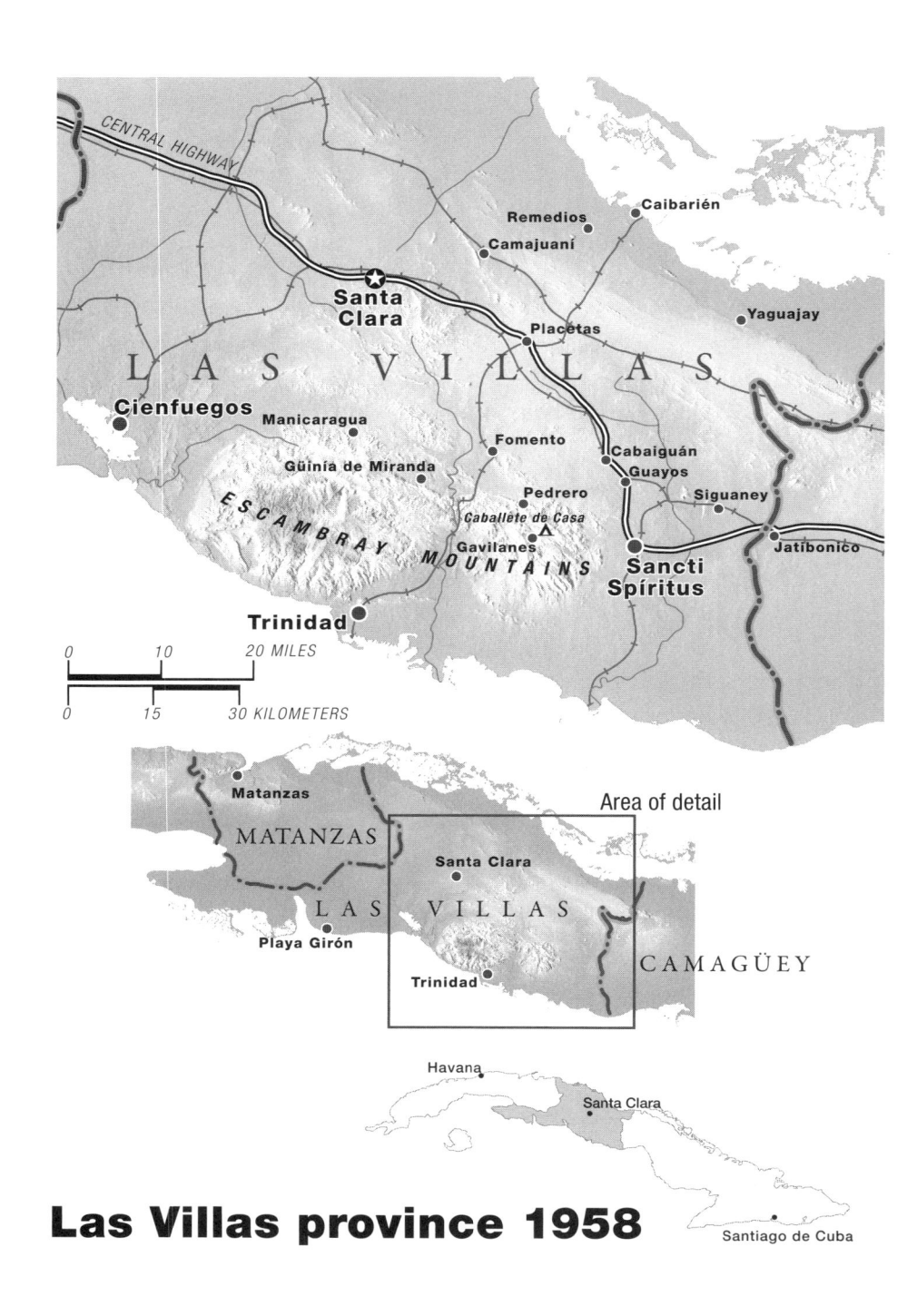

II. FIGHT TO OVERTHROW DICTATORSHIP

Spanish rule to prevent Antonio Maceo and Máximo Gómez from getting through.[7] It's like the Mariel-Majana line here in Havana province. These were systems of fortifications built by the Spanish to prevent passage of invading columns of independence fighters.

With all the water from the hurricane, Batista's troops thought that nobody would be coming through. So we made it without problems.

We reached the Escambray mountains on October 16. When we got there, Che promoted me to captain.

WATERS: When you left Jíbaro, did you think it would take you a month and a half to reach the Escambray?

ZAYAS: The plan was to cover the distance in two days in trucks, to surprise Batista's army by reaching Las Villas in forty-eight hours. That was the idea.

What happened?

The first hurricane hit before we even got to the trucks, and they got stuck in the rain and mud. So we decided to go on foot. At Camagüey we tried to get a boat but weren't able to do that either. At one point we did commandeer two trucks, but after only a few kilometers we ran into an ambush at Cuatro Compañeros. We again had to continue on foot. None of the steps we'd taken to get to the Escambray faster worked. It took us forty-seven days.

It was an exhausting march. Men were really completely

---

7. During the 1895–98 Cuban independence war, the Spanish army built a broad belt across the center of the island, about two hundred yards wide and fifty miles long, to prevent the independence forces, which were based in the east, from crossing into western Cuba. Known as the *trocha*, it included various types of fortifications, trenches, a maze of barbed wire, and a military railway line. With help from local peasants, however, invasion columns of the Cuban liberation army were able to cross the trocha easily.

drained, without food. We lacked supplies of all kinds, including extra clothing and shoes. Our feet were in terrible shape from being constantly wet, and we didn't even have a change of socks. Some men simply stopped marching. They no longer wanted to continue. They preferred to be killed by the army rather than to continue marching under those conditions—and that's what happened, the army did kill them.

"If even one person can fulfill the mission," Che said, "it shows that someone who really wants to do it *can*." I knew Che would be one of those. He was determined to carry out the mission Fidel had given him. If we'd advanced by truck, maybe we would have fallen into an ambush and none of us would have made it. If we'd done it in forty-eight hours, perhaps we wouldn't have weeded out the quitters, those who didn't have the willpower to continue. Perhaps we would never have been able to measure the capacities of those who did.

WATERS: When Che's Column 8 arrived in the Escambray, you faced some very substantial political problems. Fidel had designated Che as head of all the rebel forces there, but you had to bring them together. And you had to deal with the revolutionary pretenders and thugs of the "Second National Front of the Escambray."[8] What was your experience in this?

ZAYAS: The Second National Front of the Escambray was an organization led by Eloy Gutiérrez Menoyo and William Morgan. Morgan, an American, later joined the counterrevolutionary bands in the Escambray. He was captured, tried, and convicted of being a CIA agent, and executed. But we didn't know any of that at the time.

Che had a difficult assignment to carry out. The Second

---

8. See glossary, Second National Front of the Escambray.

Front insisted that it alone had control of the Escambray. When we arrived in the Escambray, for example, we saw a sign saying the area belonged to the Second National Front of the Escambray—that we couldn't go through that area. There were similar signs at various other spots.

At one point, they had even disarmed leaders of the July 26 forces, including Víctor Bordón, and carried out operations against the Rebel Army. The Revolutionary Directorate's forces had been shunted onto a little patch of land. The Popular Socialist Party, which also had a group fighting in Las Villas, was practically fleeing from the Second Front, which had confiscated their weapons. When Che arrived, leaders of the Second Front thought they'd continue as before.

The first thing Che did was send for one of the Second Front's officers. He wanted to explain the aim of our presence in the Escambray and show he was ready to talk to them. Che went to their camp and spoke with one of the Second Front's local commanders. By luck, I was there too.

These people were walking around in the Escambray as if there were no war going on, in good clothes, even white shirts, perfectly clean. Meanwhile, there was an army garrison in the Escambray that hadn't been taken. Actually, there were several. But in that particular area, there was a garrison in Güinía de Miranda, fourteen kilometers from Manicaragua, in the hills.

Che was inside a little hut meeting with one of the Second Front commanders. I was outside by the door, leaning against the wall, so I could see the guy talking to Che. At one point that officer became so abusive toward Che that I released the safety on my Garand (wherever we went in the Escambray, we always kept a bullet in the chamber, with the safety on). "If he makes a wrong move, I'll fire," I said to myself. He was telling Che that he and his four hundred shotguns had accomplished more than Che had, and in any case, they had nothing to learn from Che.

"Look," Che responded, "if I have to use my weapon against our own compañeros, I'll put it down and won't fight any more. I've come here to fight the Batista army, the army of the tyranny that's massacring the Cuban people, not compañeros who are supposed to be revolutionaries." Che then posed the question: "Why haven't you taken the garrison at Güinía de Miranda, when it's right here?"

"Bah, we'll take it. That's easy."

"OK, you have five days," Che told him.

"No problem, we'll take it."

Five days came and went. And the garrison had still not been taken. So off we went to our first battle in the Escambray.

We took the army garrison at Güinía de Miranda. We took it thanks to a bazooka that my squad had. Initially the man with the bazooka fired at the garrison from inside a room, but it shook him so violently he was nearly killed. When you fire a bazooka from inside like that, the recoil is like a missile. So I took it away from him.

Che and I took the bazooka through a little marabú thicket, to a point about thirty meters from the garrison. It was 4:30 a.m. and still dark. We had a problem, however. The shells were damp from all the water during the trip. You'd pull the trigger, and sometimes nothing happened. Then suddenly—boom! Out came the shell.

Since it was still dark, one person had to aim the bazooka and the other one fired. I held it and Che pulled the trigger. Then Che aimed and I pulled the trigger. On one of those attempts, with me aiming and Che pulling the trigger, the shot went off and the shell went through a window of the garrison, exploding inside a room. There was a big dust cloud. They surrendered on the spot. We went in and got all the weapons—Garands—and took the soldiers prisoner. It was a little after 4:30 a.m.

That's how we took the garrison. We had two dead and several wounded.

The next day, the Second Front people rode around the area on horseback telling everyone *they* had taken the garrison. But that didn't bother us. We were interested in the weapons and with eliminating a garrison in the Escambray.

KOPPEL: What eventually happened to the Second Front?

ZAYAS: They wanted to overthrow Batista to put themselves in power—a change of government, not a revolution. They were scoundrels. Perhaps they were a little less murderous than Batista, but just look at what happened after the victory, when they took up arms against the revolution in the Escambray.

After January 1, when we arrived in Havana, there wasn't a single soldier in the ranks of the Second Front; they were all officers! They took rooms at the Hotel Capri, one of the infamous playgrounds of American mobsters. Just imagine!

WATERS: What relations did you have with other revolutionary forces in the Escambray?

ZAYAS: One of the biggest achievements was the Pedrero Pact, where the Revolutionary Directorate, led by Faure Chomón, reached agreement with the July 26 Movement to join forces and fight together.

The Popular Socialist Party had a small platoon under the command of Pompilio Viciedo, and they placed themselves under Che's orders. The biggest PSP group in Las Villas was in the Yaguajay area in the north, where Camilo was. It was led by Félix Torres, who immediately put himself under Camilo's command.

There were also forces of the July 26 Movement led by Víctor Bordón, who put themselves under Che's command.

WATERS: When you arrived in the Escambray in mid-October, you weren't expecting to win the war in a matter of weeks or months. But every major garrison in Las Villas had fallen, and less than two and a half months later Batista had fled.

ZAYAS: It was a lightning campaign.

We began by attacking the garrisons in and around the Escambray. The Batista army in that area launched an offensive toward Pedrero from three directions. Each of these was repulsed.

Then in early December 1958 we ourselves went on the offensive.

One of the important battles occurred in Santa Lucía, a battle fought by my platoon alone. We captured the entire forward detachment of an approaching company. We took ten Garands, four machine guns—three Brownings and a .30 caliber gun—and about seven thousand bullets. They had eleven dead and four wounded. That really demoralized them.

The arms we captured allowed us to reinforce Bordón's platoon, which had really poor weapons, in order to attack an airstrip in the town of Fomento. There, on our side, Sergio Soto died heroically.

After the battle of Santa Lucía, Che ordered me to head toward Fomento, which we attacked and took in forty-eight hours. That was December 18. Fomento was the first town in Las Villas to be liberated.

We immediately then attacked Cabaiguán, which we captured on December 23 after less than forty-eight hours of combat. We took Placetas on December 23 too, and continued on to Remedios. By December 26, Remedios and Caibarién

II. FIGHT TO OVERTHROW DICTATORSHIP

both fell. Caibarién was taken by Vaquerito[9] and Che, with the squad under the command of Ramón Pardo Guerra.

Ramiro Valdés and Armando Acosta were sent to Guayos, Sancti Spíritus, and Jatibonico, and after taking these towns they headed to Ciego de Ávila.

Placetas, Remedios, and Caibarién were real battles. They lasted from twenty-four to forty-eight hours. By the end, the army was in full retreat throughout Las Villas; it no longer fought. When it found out our troops were coming, it would retreat. When we reached Santa Clara it was different; wherever the army held a position the fighting was fierce.

Meanwhile in the north, Camilo's column was attacking Yaguajay. And in the Sierra Maestra, the forces of Fidel, Raúl, and Almeida were closing in on Santiago de Cuba.

On December 27 our forces in Las Villas were back together, ready to enter the city of Santa Clara. That was the great battle, the decisive one.

We entered Santa Clara on December 28, with four hundred combatants under Che's direct command. Che sent Víctor Bordón with his forces to Santo Domingo, to block reinforcements being sent from Havana.

We were well armed, with plenty of ammunition. We had trucks. My platoon brought a truck full of ammunition and another packed with arms.

We sent for a hundred more combatants who were in the school at Caballete de Casa—above Gavilanes, in a very isolated area of the Escambray. That's something Che always did: set up a school. It was a center for recruitment and training of new recruits. Those one hundred were sent for—and given weapons—to come fight in Santa Clara.

We employed tactics in Santa Clara that were new to us: ur-

9. See glossary, Roberto Rodríguez.

COUNCIL OF STATE OFFICE OF HISTORICAL AFFAIRS

As Rebel Army fronts under Fidel Castro's command in eastern Cuba closed in on Santiago de Cuba in late December 1958, the forces led by Che Guevara took control of Cuba's fourth-largest city, Santa Clara in central Cuba. Batista fled the country and the dictatorship collapsed. "We had the support of virtually the whole population," Zayas says. Townspeople "brought us cars, and we parked them crossways in the street to block the army's tanks."

Above, cars parked by residents to block streets. **Below,** armored train with government troops derailed by Rebel Army forces during battle.

COUNCIL OF STATE OFFICE OF HISTORICAL AFFAIRS

II. FIGHT TO OVERTHROW DICTATORSHIP 95

ban combat. Che prepared us to take the city street by street. The army regiment stationed in Santa Clara had about eight or ten tanks. So townspeople brought us cars and parked them crossways in the middle of the street, to block the tanks.

We had the support of virtually the entire population.

An important moment in the battle was the capture of the armored train. It was holed up—with soldiers inside—on Loma de Capiro, a strategic hill on the edge of Santa Clara. This was a train headed to Oriente. The government was giving out the story that it was carrying the Engineer Corps, that it was full of engineers and railwaymen. But really it was carrying four hundred soldiers.

So Che sent me to attack them. When we began climbing Loma de Capiro, they retreated into the train. We had acquired a bulldozer on the highway from Camajuaní to Santa Clara, and we pulled up the railroad tracks as we went up the hill. When the train started backing up, it derailed. Pardo Guerra played an important role in securing the surrender of the forces there.

Civilians made Molotov cocktails and hurled them at the rail cars, attacking the train alongside our forces. The four hundred soldiers inside surrendered. We gathered up machine guns, bullets, bazookas, mortars, artillery, everything.

Che sent many of these weapons and munitions to Camilo in Yaguajay, where his forces were tied down fighting the garrison. Camilo fought the troops in Yaguajay for eleven days, during which Che went there two or three times.

These weapons also helped us enter central Santa Clara, where we took the police station, the jail, the provincial government palace, the Hotel Cloris. We surrounded the headquarters of the "little horses"—the motorcycle cops—and captured the courthouse. Forces from the March 13 Directorate also took part in the operation.

WATERS: What stands out in your memory of that battle?

ZAYAS: One thing I remember took place on the street leading to the back of the regimental headquarters.

Che was on Independence Street, perpendicular to the one I was on. He was making a type of Molotov cocktail, using those big five-gallon glass water bottles, twenty-five liters. We used them to take out tanks. You'd go to the second floor of a house, and when the tank passed below, you'd drop the jug so it broke on top of the tank, covering it with flammable liquid. Then you'd toss a burning bottle to set the tank on fire.

Che gave me one of those jugs, and I lugged it up the stairs to the second floor of a building overlooking the street behind the regiment. I settled in to wait, since that was the street the tanks were supposed to come down. Che posted other people on Independence Street, in case the tanks went that way.

A tank came down the street and got to about half a block from where I was. Luckily for the soldiers in the tank, it started to break down, spewing out a huge cloud of smoke. They put it in reverse, turned around, and headed back to the regiment. I never got a chance to drop my jug on them.

Meanwhile, Vaquerito was ordered to take the police station. Vaquerito, whose real name was Roberto Rodríguez, was the head of what we called the Suicide Squad, selected from the fighters who were the most courageous, who had the highest combat morale. He was killed in this attack. But the police station was taken and we captured two tanks.

Che sent a platoon headed by Miguel Álvarez, together with combatants from the Revolutionary Directorate, to take Garrison 31 and the headquarters of the "little horses." Rogelio Acevedo with his platoon went to take the courthouse.

Che had me take my platoon to the center of town. In the Escambray, my entire platoon had a little over thirty men. But

"Cuba's wealth was handed over to foreign masters. The best farmland, the largest sugar mills, the basic industries, the railroads, the banks passed into the iron grip of US monopoly capital."

FIDEL CASTRO, DECEMBER 1975

LIBRARY OF CONGRESS

COURTESY YOUTH CLUB JESÚS MENÉNDEZ

Top, workers and children load sugarcane for transport to mill, early 20th century. Relations of production changed little until victory of 1959 revolution. **Bottom,** US-owned Chaparra sugar mill (pre-1959, today Jesús Menéndez), near Zayas's home in Puerto Padre in eastern Cuba. By late 1930s, more than 80 percent of sugar in Cuba was produced in foreign-owned mills, primarily US, Spanish, and Canadian.

"The one social force capable of emancipating the country from oppression was the working class. Moreover, it was the only force capable of supporting us against the imperialist power oppressing our country." FIDEL CASTRO, DECEMBER 1975

BOHEMIA

COUNCIL OF STATE OFFICE OF HISTORICAL AFFAIRS

Facing page, top, striking sugar workers in Santo Domingo, central Cuba, 1955. "It was a powerful strike," Zayas said. "Over 200,000 workers walked out of US- and Cuban-owned mills." Strikers were resisting attempt to cut wages. Drawing support from students and others, strike took on political character, dealt blow to Batista dictatorship, and pushed back pay cut substantially. **Bottom left,** US sailors urinated on Havana statue of Cuban national hero José Martí, March 1949. **Bottom right,** US ambassador sought to defuse protests against this insult by sending wreath to monument. **Center,** demonstrators display burned wreath.
This page, top, peasant families being evicted by plantation owners, Camagüey province, 1942. **Bottom,** rural schoolhouse, 1950s.

"Despite setbacks suffered at the beginning of the revolutionary war, Fidel's firmness and tenacity, the determination never to give up, sustained the guerrilla fighters." RAÚL CASTRO, JULY 1961

COUNCIL OF STATE OFFICE OF HISTORICAL AFFAIRS

COUNCIL OF STATE OFFICE OF HISTORICAL AFFAIRS

Top, Fidel Castro (center) and other combatants meet with peasants in Sierra Maestra, early 1957. Throughout war, Alfonso Zayas says, Rebel Army leaders met with peasants "to explain the objectives of the revolution, including an agrarian reform that would guarantee them land." **Bottom,** Frank País (center, in white) with defense attorney and fellow defendants during April 1957 trial of *Granma* expeditionaries and participants in November 30, 1956, uprising in Santiago de Cuba, of which País was central organizer. From left: Carlos Chaín, attorney José Grillo Longoria, Jorge Serguera, País, and two others (unidentified). Uprising was timed to support landing of *Granma* yacht, carrying 82 combatants led by Castro, to begin revolutionary war against US-backed Batista tyranny.

COURTESY ALFONSO ZAYAS

COUNCIL OF STATE OFFICE OF HISTORICAL AFFAIRS

GRANMA

Top, a few of 51 members of Rebel Army's first reinforcement detachment, the *Marabuzaleros*, who in March 1957 more than tripled the number of combatants. In front: Guillermo Domínguez; behind, from left: Raúl Castro Mercader, Orlando Pupo, Alfonso Zayas. **Left,** shoe repair shop in El Hombrito camp, where, under Che Guevara's command, workshops were organized to make weapons, leather goods, uniforms, bread, and more. From station nearby, Radio Rebelde began broadcasting. **Right,** rebels at El Hombrito putting out mimeographed *El Cubano Libre* newspaper.

In October 1958 "we began by attacking garrisons in and around the Escambray. Then we went on the offensive across Las Villas. It was a lightning campaign." ALFONSO ZAYAS

COURTESY ALFONSO ZAYAS

Top, Zayas (second from left) and other combatants after liberation of Placetas in Las Villas, December 1958. At center is Alberto Fernández, who in 1966–67 was part of revolutionary column led by Che Guevara in Bolivia, where he was known as Pacho.
Bottom, "Ñico López" School for Recruits, organized by Guevara at Caballete de Casa, deep in Escambray mountains. Photo shows December 1958 commemoration of 19th century independence leader Antonio Maceo's death in combat. "Wherever Che went, he always set up a school to train new recruits," Zayas says.

GRANMA

GRANMA

Top, Rebel Army Column 8 heading to Santa Clara, December 27, 1958. Liberation of fourth-largest city of Cuba dealt decisive defeat to dictatorship. In face of strengthening mass insurrection and imminent fall of Santiago de Cuba, Batista fled the island January 1.
Bottom, revolutionary troops led by Fidel Castro greeted in Havana, January 8, 1959, as "Freedom Caravan" crossed the country from liberated Santiago.

"On January 1, 1959, with a firm base of workers and peasants, we began to storm the heavens."

RAÚL CASTRO, JULY 1961

NATIONAL INSTITUTE OF AGRARIAN REFORM

BOHEMIA

Land reform and expropriation of major capitalist enterprises were defining acts of Cuba's socialist revolution. In May 1959 the new government gave 100,000 peasants title to land they worked. In response, U.S. rulers stepped up efforts to overthrow the revolutionary government, and mass mobilizations of working people backed expropriation of landlords and capitalists. **Top,** peasants establishing farm cooperative in Cárdenas, Cuba, early 1960s. **Bottom,** militia members in front of recently nationalized Cuban Telephone Company, August 1960.

GRANMA

Revolutionary tribunals judged hundreds of Batista regime's murderers and torturers. "This may have been the only revolution in which war criminals were tried and brought to justice, not dragged through the streets," Fidel Castro later noted. **Top,** Batista henchman Jesús Sosa Blanco (standing at right) on trial, February 1959. **Bottom,** woman testifying about Sosa Blanco's murder of family members.

GRANMA

"After the revolution voluntary labor was necessary for every harvest. There were no longer a million unemployed workers whose families would starve if they didn't cut cane." ALFONSO ZAYAS

PRENSA LATINA

Top, volunteers mobilizing to cut sugarcane, 1963. Bottom, workers operating harvester in 1970s. Mechanization of cane cutting, first developed in Cuba, freed a million workers from back-breaking labor.

GRANMA

LIBORIO NOVAL

Top, women eager to participate in revolution were organized to do so. Here women keep factory production going during defense mobilization when Washington threatened to invade at time of October 1962 "missile" crisis **Center,** 1960, building road through Zapata swamp, an isolated area in central Cuba that includes Bay of Pigs, undertaken as part of revolutionary government's programs for economic development and defense preparedness. **Bottom,** Che Guevara (right) often joined voluntary labor brigades such as this one building houses, 1961.

"Had Cuban forces not arrived in time, the independence struggle of the Angolan people would have been thwarted. The South African military would have captured Luanda in November 1975."

ALFONSO ZAYAS

The defeat of South Africa's army at Cuito Cuanavale, Angola, in 1988, Nelson Mandela said, was "a turning point in the struggle to free the continent and our country from the scourge of apartheid." **Top,** Che Guevara (left) meets with Agostinho Neto (right) and other leaders of Popular Movement for the Liberation of Angola (MPLA) during 1965 tour of Africa, which laid foundations for Cuba's support to liberation movements there. **Bottom,** Angolans celebrate installation of their own government on first day of independence from Portuguese colonial rule, November 11, 1975. The new government asked Cuba for military aid in repelling assault by apartheid regime. Over 16 years, nearly 400,000 Cuban internationalist volunteers, including Zayas, fought alongside Angolans resisting multiple invasions.

Top, first group of Cuban instructors after arrival in Angola, October 1975. **Bottom,** South African soldiers captured by Cuban and Angolan forces, December 1975. "They were irrefutable proof," an Angolan daily said, that South Africa had invaded Angola, a fact the apartheid regime denied.

"Those who once enslaved men and sent them to the Americas perhaps never imagined that one of the countries that received the slaves would one day send their fighters to struggle for freedom in Africa."

FIDEL CASTRO, APRIL 1976

GRANMA

GRANMA

Top, Cuban internationalist combatants in southern Angola. **Bottom,** March 1976, Conakry, Guinea: Fidel Castro meets with Agostinho Neto (right) and with presidents of the two African countries that also sent troops to aid Angola, Luís Cabral of Guinea-Bissau and Ahmed Sékou Touré of Guinea (first and second from left). With support of the Cuban volunteers, Angolan army turned back apartheid regime's 15-year aggression, Zayas explains. When he first went to Angola in December 1975, "South African forces, backed by Washington, were just 300 kilometers from the capital city of Luanda."

JON HILLSON/MILITANT

COURTESY GERARDO HERNÁNDEZ

Top, members of Cuban women's antiaircraft artillery unit, May 1989, after return from Angola following defeat of South African invasion. **Bottom,** Cuban-Angolan reconnaissance platoon in Cabinda province, Angola, 1989–90. Platoon was led by Gerardo Hernández (center, second row), who today is one of five Cuban revolutionaries framed by Washington and serving long sentences in U.S. prisons.

"Under capitalism, when work is intensified, the boss gets more surplus value. Here it's the workers who gain. That's what the Cuban Revolution changed half a century ago." ALFONSO ZAYAS

TERRY COGGAN/MILITANT

Above, workers in minibrigades build housing in Cuba, late 1980s, in response to leadership initiatives known as the rectification process. Many thousands volunteered to construct homes, schools, child-care centers, clinics, and other needed facilities, while coworkers picked up slack for them on their jobs.

In response to drastic food shortages following collapse of trade with Soviet Union in early 1990s, programs were initiated in Cuba to boost agricultural production. **Top,** urban vegetable farms such as this one in Havana increased supply of fresh produce in cities. **Center,** market run by Youth Army of Labor (EJT), 1995. EJT, which Zayas helped lead, brings produce into cities and sells at prices lower than other markets.

After 2002, some 90 sugar mills with antiquated equipment were closed and much of land turned over to raising vegetables, fruits, and livestock. Many former sugar workers went back to school while receiving full salaries. **Bottom,** former sugar workers, who became teachers at Camilo Cienfuegos School for Further Education in Santa Cruz del Norte, February 2007.

"Cuba has resisted and continues to resist. By doing so, it provides an example to the world that revolution is possible, that working people can struggle and win." **ALFONSO ZAYAS**

JACOB PERASSO/MILITANT

ASSOCIATION OF COMBATANTS OF THE CUBAN REVOLUTION

Top, youth march in Havana November 27, 2009, organized by Federation of University Students (FEU) to honor medical students killed on this date in 1871 by Spanish colonial regime. Banner quotes former FEU leader and revolutionary martyr José Antonio Echeverría, "If we fall, our blood will point the way to freedom."
Bottom, Col. Jesús Almeida Hernández speaks from floor at 1993 meeting in Havana of Association of Combatants of the Cuban Revolution. In first full row, from right, are Generals Lino Carreras, Enrique Carreras, and Arnaldo Tamayo.

Top, Guiteras sugar mill (Delicias before the revolution) in Las Tunas province after hurricanes Gustav, Ike, and Paloma in 2008, which caused $10 billion in damage in Cuba. **Center,** workers rebuild housing in Las Tunas. Through efforts of government and mobilizations of working people, tens of thousands of damaged factories, homes, schools, and other facilities, including Guiteras mill, were rapidly repaired or rebuilt. **Bottom,** Cuban doctor, one of hundreds serving in Haiti after 2010 earthquake, treats cholera patients in L'Estère, northern Haiti, October 2010. "Today in Cuba no one younger than 50 knows firsthand the horror of capitalist reality," says Zayas. "But those who volunteer for internationalist missions see what Cuba was like before the revolution. They're learning about capitalism, about the exploitation of man by man."

"The courage and integrity shown by our Five Heroes is an example to millions around the world."

ALFONSO ZAYAS

Five Cuban revolutionaries are today serving draconian sentences in US prisons due to their actions in defense of the revolution. The frame-up charges included "conspiracy to commit espionage" and "conspiracy to commit murder." Case has generated a broad international protest campaign. **Top left,** Gerardo Hernández (on right) with other Cuban volunteer combatants in Angola. **Top right,** Ramón Labañino (center) visited by his father, Holmes (right), and brother Holmito in McCreary federal prison in Kentucky, April 2010. **Inset photos,** from left, Fernando González in Angola; René González in Angola; Antonio Guerrero in U.S. penitentiary in Florence, Colorado, with his painting of Adriana Pérez, wife of Gerardo, who has not been allowed to visit her husband in 12 years. **Below,** mass rally in Havana demands Washington release the five, May 2010.

II. FIGHT TO OVERTHROW DICTATORSHIP

in Santa Clara there were squads in the platoon that alone had forty. We'd begun incorporating the militia, local people.

Che ordered me to select a small platoon to give to Pacho—Alberto Fernández Monte de Oca, who later died with Che in Bolivia—to capture the provincial government center, city hall, which was right across from Vidal Park.

After city hall was taken, Che gave me the mission to take the Hotel Cloris, today the Santa Clara Libre, which was also on the park. There were twelve enemy snipers in the upper floors. I positioned my platoon around the hotel, so we could enter from below and set fire to everything.

It was about 11:00 at night, and I saw a tank coming toward us. Kiko—Alberto Martínez Rosales—a combatant who had made the march from Oriente, was driving. Kiko had been a tractor driver, so he knew how to operate a tank—a tank is just like a tractor. When I went over to the tank, I saw Che was inside.

"Che, what are you doing in there!" I said. "Don't you know our people now have bazookas and antitank guns?"

"I know where everyone is," he replied, "and they won't fire at me."

Kiko told me there was another tank over at the command post. I too knew how to drive tractors with treads, which I learned as a boy. So I went and took the tank and drove it to the corner of Vidal Park. I opened fire on the upper stories, enabling our people to get into the hotel from below. Inside the hotel today, if you look up you can still see a few holes from the tank's .30 caliber machine guns.

When our people reached the first-floor lobby, we set a fire—curtains, furniture, everything—so smoke would rise up the stairwells and elevator shaft. But when we learned there were a hundred civilians suffocating on the fifth floor, we put out the fire. Then we brought those people down and got them outside, before setting the fire again. A little later, we heard the army snipers shouting from above. Smoke had filled the spaces where they were, and they thought the entire hotel was on fire. So they surrendered.

This was about 2:00 a.m. on January 1. Right around that time, as we were soon to learn, Batista was fleeing Cuba.

Having captured the Hotel Cloris, there was now nothing left but the regimental garrison, which had some two thousand soldiers. But with Batista gone, we started talks with people from the regiment.

At the head of the regiment was Colonel Joaquín Casillas Lumpuy, who in 1948, as a captain, had murdered Jesús Menéndez, the sugar workers leader, in Manzanillo. Casillas took off for Havana, leaving his second-in-command in charge, and the garrison fell. He had put on civilian clothes but our people in the area around Santo Domingo recognized Casillas and took him prisoner. As they were bringing him back to Santa Clara, he jumped one of our fighters to try to take his rifle away, and a combatant from my platoon shot and killed him.

Meanwhile, Che had received an order from Fidel: advance on Havana and take the La Cabaña army fortress there.

PART III

Soldier of the Revolution

III. Soldier of the Revolution

With the establishment of the new revolutionary government in early 1959, the Rebel Army and July 26 Movement immediately began implementing the program they had been explaining, and around which they had been organizing, from the outset of the struggle. During the opening months of 1959, with broad backing among the Cuban people, revolutionary tribunals were created to try hundreds of the most infamous murderers and torturers of the Batista regime. The new government slashed the exorbitant electricity and phone rates that working people paid to the US-owned utility monopolies and declared illegal the multiple forms of state-sanctioned racial discrimination against blacks.

The most deepgoing measure of the first year of the revolution was the agrarian reform law of May 17, which set a limit of 30 caballerías (some 1,000 acres) on individual landholdings. Implementation of the law resulted in the revolutionary confiscation of vast cane fields and cattle ranches—most owned by wealthy US families or by corporations they controlled. These lands passed into the hands of the new government and became state property. The law granted sharecroppers, tenant farmers, and squatters title to the land they tilled. Some 100,000 peasant families received deeds.

Among the plantations taken over from their US owners were Chaparra and Delicias, near Zayas's hometown of Puerto Padre.

With the agrarian reform, as Raúl Castro later remarked, the revolution crossed the Rubicon. Bourgeois forces in Cuba and abroad realized the Rebel Army–led revolutionary government was serious about carrying through a program in the interests of the vast majority. It could not be bought off, threatened, or diverted. The propertied classes accelerated their efforts to overthrow the new government. Washington initiated a course to support that effort that remains in place today, more than half a century later.

From August through October 1960, working people in Cuba responded to each step in the escalation of the US rulers' armed assaults and economic sabotage with mass mobilizations backing the nationalization of the holdings of the major US-owned companies. The expropriation of large Cuban-owned capitalist enterprises followed. By the second anniversary of the fall of the dictatorship, Cuba's workers and farmers had opened the door to a socialist revolution.

The new property relations enabled Cuba's working people to begin remaking the economic and social relations inherited from capitalism and imperialist domination.

Illiteracy was wiped out in a single year, as a hundred thousand young teachers enthusiastically fanned out across the country to teach every adult Cuban to read and write. Schools were established and public education became available to all. Clinics and homes were built. Access to electricity was extended to working people in city and countryside. Sugar workers no longer went hungry during the "dead time," as shortages of labor power—not a vast army of unemployed—marked working-class efforts at economic and social reconstruction. The goal was for every Cuban to become a productive worker. As women mobilized to participate, they began to make major gains in education and employment. Health care was organized for all, regardless of ability to pay.

Drawing on deep popular support for the revolutionary measures, the Rebel Army increased its size, combat readiness,

III. SOLDIER OF THE REVOLUTION

and professionalism to defend the new state power and its conquests. Cuban working people flooded the ranks of the voluntary Revolutionary National Militia and the Revolutionary National Police, and the Rebel Army became the Revolutionary Armed Forces (FAR) of Cuba.

The capacity of working people to defend their new power was proved at Playa Girón in April 1961, when they decisively defeated the US-organized invasion at the Bay of Pigs. It was tested and confirmed once again in October 1962, when Cuban toilers and their government prevented a threatened US invasion during the so-called Missile Crisis, and as they organized between 1961 and 1965 to defeat US-organized counterrevolutionary bands in the Escambray mountains.

To accomplish these tasks—far more difficult than taking power—the revolutionary leadership drew on the proven capacities and discipline of fighters, men and women like Alfonso Zayas. In the five decades since 1959, these soldiers of the revolution, from several generations, have taken on whatever needed to be done.

WATERS: Did you leave Santa Clara for Havana with Che on January 1?

ZAYAS: No. Che had me stay to help organize the column. By then it was very large, with almost two thousand combatants, and it had to be taken to Havana. Che went on ahead with a group that included his escort of Antonio Núñez Jiménez, Oscar Fernández Mell, Harry Villegas, Leonardo Tamayo, Alberto Castellanos, and others. On January 2, they took over the La Cabaña fortress, which dominates the entrance to Havana harbor. We arrived at 3:00 a.m. on January 3.

As soon as Che occupied the garrison at La Cabaña, he put all the soldiers and officers of Batista's army quartered there on leave for a month. The soldiers' weapons were to be left behind, as well as all other state property. They left with just the clothes on their backs and a few personal items. The officers were allowed to keep their revolvers. A month later, when they came back from leave, they learned they'd all been discharged from the armed forces.

Che put me in charge of the military prison at La Cabaña. Running a jail was something I knew absolutely nothing about.

There weren't many prisoners at first, but they quickly started to arrive. On January 1, in response to Fidel's call for a general strike and a popular insurrection, police stations and garrisons all across the country had been taken, and in the days that followed many of the regime's henchmen were captured. I'm talking about the ones who didn't escape with Batista—the ones who had to pay for their crimes. From all directions, at all hours of the day and night, patrol cars began to arrive at La Cabaña. In the end, more than a thousand of these thugs and murderers had been turned over.

They included Hernando Hernández, the head of the national police, as well as Jesús Sosa Blanco, Merob Sosa, Pelayo Alayón, and Pedro Morejón. There was also Ricardo José Grau, a general related to former Cuban president Grau San Martín, and other officers of the navy, the police, and the army. Ernesto de la Fe, Batista's mafia-style information minister, was brought in. There were all kinds of people who had committed every type of atrocity.

One of the most notorious criminals captured and tried was Jesús Sosa Blanco. This was a man who had set fire to houses with families inside. So many victims demanded to testify against Sosa Blanco that the trial was held in the Ciudad Deportiva stadium. It was open to the public and televised.

WATERS: In the United States and elsewhere at that time, a

III. SOLDIER OF THE REVOLUTION

> This may have been the only revolution in which the main war criminals were tried and brought to justice, the only revolution that didn't rob or steal, didn't drag people through the streets, didn't take revenge, didn't take justice into its own hands. No one was ever lynched here. Not that some people wouldn't have liked to. Because the crimes committed by Batista's thugs and henchmen, those people who thought they could get away with anything, had been horrible. And if there were no lynchings, no bloodbaths it was because of our insistence and our promise: "War criminals will be brought to justice and punished, as examples."
>
> FIDEL CASTRO
> 2006[*]

campaign attacking these trials as violations of human rights began immediately. The charge was that the revolution simply executed its enemies without due process.

ZAYAS: All kinds of accusations were made by enemies of the revolution. But no one was executed without having a trial with all established guarantees.

Charges were brought against these criminals by the victims of their outrages, including some whose families had been murdered. Torture victims came to testify: "This man tortured me. See the scar on my back from the beatings." Or "That man tore out my fingernails." Some victims had had their eyes gouged out.

As prison chief at La Cabaña, I attended the trials of these murderers. I was also on the tribunal that judged Alayón and Morejón.

[*] Fidel Castro, *My Life* (New York: Allen Lane, 2007), pp. 220–21.

COURTESY ALFONSO ZAYAS

"Enemies of the revolution accused us of violating the human rights of former Batista henchmen who committed atrocities," says Zayas. "But no one was executed without a trial with all the established guarantees. Victims of their outrages brought charges against these criminals. We protected them from being lynched in the street by the population."

Above, Alfonso Zayas (left foreground) in 1959. Zayas was first director of La Cabaña prison in Havana, where Batista regime's hated torturers and murderers were held awaiting trial. He is shaking hands with fellow Rebel Army combatant César Hernández.

Below, Zayas graduating from advanced course for military officers, 1967. From left: Zayas, José Ramón Fernández, Fidel Castro (handing him diploma), and Juan Almeida. After graduating, Zayas took assignment to lead work of Communist Party in Holguín province.

COURTESY ALFONSO ZAYAS

III. SOLDIER OF THE REVOLUTION

WATERS: In the book *Cien horas con Fidel* [One Hundred Hours with Fidel], journalist Ignacio Ramonet asks Fidel about these trials.[1] Fidel's answer was very good. Some mistakes were made in the way a few of the trials were conducted, Fidel said—mistakes the revolutionary leadership rapidly corrected. But the revolutionary tribunals, he explained, were established precisely *to prevent* the criminals from being dragged through the streets by angry mobs and executed without due process. The truth is the opposite of what Washington charged. The revolutionary tribunals brought order and the rule of law.

ZAYAS: Had these individuals been released, they would have been lynched in the street. We had to protect them from the population. The people wanted justice for the deaths of their family members, their loved ones.

KOPPEL: How long did you have the assignment as head of the prison?

ZAYAS: Three months. After that I went to Santa Clara with a battalion of the Rebel Army's Tactical Force.

While I was in Santa Clara, Fidel summoned me. He gave me the assignment to go with my battalion to what was then still called the Isle of Pines—it's now the Isle of Youth—to guard it and work on a reforestation plan, planting citrus orchards and other fruit trees. "You'll see what this island will become in twenty years," Fidel said at the end of our discussion.

So off I went to carry out that twenty-year assignment.

When the battle of Playa Girón took place in April 1961, I was on the Isle of Youth at the head of an infantry battalion.

WATERS: What happened after Playa Girón?

ZAYAS: After barely a year on the Isle of Pines, they sent me

---

1. Published in English as Fidel Castro, *My Life*.

to Matanzas to take the Basic Course for officers at the military school headed by José Ramón Fernández. He had led the main column against the invading forces at Playa Girón. I spent seven months there in 1961.

I emerged with a little training, enough to be assigned—after a stint in Pinar del Río to lead a division—to command combat units in Havana to defend the city. In Havana I served as chief of staff of UM 2350, the military unit of five thousand men permanently assigned to the city's defense. That's where I was during the October 1962 "Missile" Crisis—the head of the general staff of an infantry division in Havana.

Next they sent me to organize political education in the Western Army, which was headquartered at the military base in Managua, a little ways southeast of Havana. Each army unit had an assigned political officer. I was responsible for the political section of the Western Army until 1967, when they sent me to the Advanced Course for officers. By that time I'd been promoted to commander.

There were twelve in our class. When the course finished, Julio Camacho and I were transferred to the FAR reserves. We were assigned to civilian life, to work in the Communist Party. Camacho was sent to Pinar del Río, and I was sent to Holguín as party secretary. That was in 1968, and I was there until 1972.

When I was given this civilian assignment, I asked Raúl: "Am I losing my status in the military?"

"No," he replied. "We're either civilian or military, one or the other, depending on what's needed." So I kept on wearing my uniform.

Around that time there was a May Day celebration, attended by the secretary of the Communist Party of the Soviet Union. I went in dress uniform, impeccable, with my commander's insignia. Behind the stage before the event began,

Raúl introduced me to the Soviet leader: "Let me introduce you to the only commander who is now a party secretary and hasn't taken off his uniform." I got the message!

When I returned to Holguín, I traded my shirt and cap for a hat and a gray khaki shirt. But I kept wearing military pants.

My assignment in Holguín came at a difficult time, because the 1970 sugar harvest—the massive effort to produce ten million tons—was then being prepared.[2]

WATERS: Why was the goal of a ten-million-ton sugar harvest so important?

ZAYAS: Fidel explained it when he drew the balance sheet on our failure to reach the goal. The effort was required to meet "basic needs of the economy, for our development, to overcome and climb out of our poverty," Fidel explained in an address to the people of Cuba on July 26, 1970. He pointed out that every year we imported—and had to find a way to pay for—five million tons of fuel and more than fifty thousand tons of milk. That we needed at least a million more houses to provide every worker and farmer a decent place to live. That we lacked even the most basic machine tools for our factories and repair facilities.

WATERS: As party secretary in Holguín, what were your responsibilities for the ten million tons campaign?

---

2. In 1968 the Cuban government launched a drive to produce ten million tons of sugar in 1970. The aim was to finance agricultural diversification and industrial development, while simultaneously easing dependence on economic aid from the Soviet Union and Eastern Europe. This was a major political campaign, mobilizing voluntary labor throughout the country to prepare the fields and plant, harvest, and process the sugar. As Zayas explains, they were unable to meet the goal, bringing in 8.5 million tons, not ten. The effort led to major economic dislocations.

ZAYAS: The party's responsibilities are political, not administrative. But as party secretary, I did have to be directly involved in responding to the problems in agriculture and sugar production. The party had to involve itself in the effort. We had a command post in the countryside working alongside the compañeros who were directing the sugar industry. Our aim was to make sure everything that needed to be done was done.

Fidel set the example, being directly involved in the 1970 sugar harvest.

In sugarcane production—like any agricultural endeavor—you can't just decide to plant the cane and leave it at that. Before planting, the soil must be prepared a number of times, so the cane will grow. You must check on the possibilities for irrigation. You have to fertilize, remove weeds, provide the care necessary.

In those days that meant big popular mobilizations to plant the cane and then to cut it. The sugarcane industry wasn't yet mechanized. There were lifters to raise the cane and load it onto trucks, but almost all the cutting was still done by hand.

The agricultural labor force was no longer sufficient. The revolution had changed all that. There were no longer a million unemployed workers whose families would starve if they didn't cut cane. Popular mobilizations from different enterprises and mass organizations were necessary for every harvest. Each organization was responsible for organizing voluntary labor to help. The party had to be in the front ranks of the mobilizations—not just to cut cane, but to clear the fields, to pull weeds. It was very hard work.

The campaign for a ten-million-ton harvest in 1970 began in 1968—two years earlier. In many places we had to clear away forested areas in order to prepare the land for cane planting.

This was necessary because some of the land being planted had previously been dedicated to livestock, with wooded patches to provide shade for the cattle. Plus there were thickets of marabú, which is not easy to get rid of. In Holguín there were bulldozer brigades, whole companies of demolition specialists and engineers who dynamited tree stumps and pulled them out with bulldozers.

Irrigation systems had to be built, as well as drainage ditches, since some land being brought into production was in low-lying areas. Roads had to be built. Railroad tracks had to be laid for the cars that transported the cane. Collection centers had to be constructed. The whole sugar industry had to be modernized and expanded.

All this entailed work and planning for a huge job, and the party had to be on the front lines. In Holguín, where I was, we planted around forty thousand hectares [some ninety-nine thousand acres] of sugarcane.

WATERS: How did this compare with previous plantings?

ZAYAS: The sugar industry was already established in Holguín. But we didn't have even 50 percent of what was needed to meet the ten-million-ton goal. We had to increase the area where cane was planted. Part of the land to be cultivated, as I mentioned, had previously been used for livestock. These broad swaths of pasture were virtually undeveloped—just cattle grazing on grass. There were few paved roads, much less railroads or irrigation. All that had to be created.

WATERS: Following the failure of the effort, Fidel made a sober assessment of the reasons and the consequences. What were some of the conclusions?

ZAYAS: We created many of the necessary conditions for the ten million tons, but the change was very violent and sudden. Small industries had to expand rapidly so they could produce more. It was too big a leap.

I'll give you an example. Before the 1970 harvest, the Cristino Naranjo sugar refinery in Holguín used to produce two thousand tons a day. It was expanded so it could produce more than six thousand tons. It went from a tiny sugar mill to a gigantic one. It wasn't easy for the workers and administration to adapt to such a big change. It's not the same to work with a daily capacity of two thousand tons as it is of six thousand. The difference isn't just quantitative. Everything has to work well, and at the same time. All the gears had to mesh. And they didn't.

In 1970 we did manage to produce 8.5 million tons, a figure never before reached. The largest harvest before that had been 7.1 million in 1952. So it was an enormous leap. But we didn't make the ten million.

There were other factors, too, such as bad weather. It was a very rainy year, and rain hurts the harvest. It's not the same to cut and transport sugarcane in the rain as it is in dry weather.

Despite the great effort by the Cuban people, and despite what we achieved, it wasn't what we wanted. It took a long time to recover from the disruption of production in other sectors of the economy due to the effort.

Fidel was the guiding force in the campaign for the ten million tons. The whole Communist Party Central Committee, cadres with state and government responsibilities, mobilized to cut cane. We made a heroic effort. And Fidel took responsibility for the outcome.

WATERS: What was the political work of the party during the ten-million-ton effort? What positive and negative lessons were drawn?

ZAYAS: Political work with the population is one of our fundamental tasks. The party has to look at its own members—how they function, the example they set in the eyes of other

GRANMA

In 1970 Cuba's revolutionary leadership mobilized more than one million people in voluntary work brigades in effort to produce a record 10 million tons of sugar to finance accelerated industrialization. The harvest, while biggest in Cuba's history, fell short by .5 million tons. At the time, Zayas was first secretary of Communist Party in the eastern province of Holguín.

Above, mass rally during campaign. "Women are present in the 1970 harvest," reads banner of Federation of Cuban Women.

We've just finished waging a battle that can truly be called heroic. The heroes of that battle are represented here. The people were the heroes of that battle, the battle for the ten million tons. . . .

That effort was required for basic needs of the economy, for our development, to climb out of our poverty. Let us not forget that in spite of everything, for several years we have had an unfavorable foreign trade balance, mainly with the Soviet Union. Let us not forget that we must import more than five million tons of fuel. . . .

We import all the energy for the lights we use, for every lathe that turns, for every machine and motor of any kind. This energy replaces man in all kinds of activities; it powers collection and processing centers, moves machines, satisfies essential needs. . . .

But the heroic effort to increase production resulted in imbalances in the economy, in reduced production in other sectors. . . .

If the enemy makes use of some of the things we say and causes us deep shame, let us welcome it! The embarrassment will be welcome if we know how to turn the shame into strength, if we know how to turn the shame into a will to work, if we know how to turn the shame into dignity, and if we know how to turn it into moral strength!

FIDEL CASTRO
JULY 26, 1970[*]

---

[*] Fidel Castro, "Speech at Commemoration of Seventeenth Anniversary of Attack on Moncada Barracks." An English translation is available online at http://lanic.utexas.edu/project/castro/db/1970/19700726.html.

workers. It has to win workers who demonstrate the best qualities to join the party.

The party's job with the youth and the mass organization is primarily political. The party gives political leadership to all these forces—the CDRs, ANAP, the Federation of Cuban Women, the CTC.[3]

The 1970 sugar harvest was a good example. To carry it out, party cadres had to work with all the other organizations and agencies in order to explain what had to be done. The party had to monitor and lead every aspect of the effort.

You can't just tell someone, "We need you for a month to go do such and such a job"—cutting cane, for instance. You have to work through all the details. When that volunteer arrives, conditions have to be ready, including food and other necessities. You even have to make sure the man or woman doing the cooking prepares the food well. There's a vast array of details.

If a woman with children joins a mobilization, who'll care for her children while she's gone? Or a man with children. Who's responsible for attention to that family while he or she is mobilized? It's the same in production as for those who fulfill an internationalist mission in the armed forces. Someone has to take care of the family left behind. Who makes sure their children go to school? There's a chain of things requiring solutions.

WATERS: I'm thinking of what Fidel has raised repeatedly: not having the party intervene too much in administration instead of leading politically.

3. See glossary: Committees for the Defense of the Revolution (CDRs), National Association of Small Farmers (ANAP), Federation of Cuban Women (FMC), Central Organization of Cuban Workers (CTC).

ZAYAS: Party cadres have to ensure that the plan of a given enterprise or entity is fulfilled, and that the administrator does what needs to be done. That's different from the party acting as the administration. It's different from the party secretary becoming too heavy-handed and starting to function administratively instead of politically.

There've been many examples. The sugar harvest of 1970 was one of the most important. There was a lot of pressure to meet the goals. The provincial party secretary sometimes got so involved in the problems that he was virtually administering.

I'm speaking of myself in Holguín. I was so firmly implanted in the agricultural command post, it was almost as if I were agricultural director—even though I claimed not to be. I was so deeply involved I might as well have been one more administrator. I give that as an example of what the party fights *not* to do.

KOPPEL: After finishing your assignment as party secretary in Holguín in 1972, what did you do?

ZAYAS: I was assigned to work as director of agricultural mechanization in Havana province. At the time the province encompassed what was until 2010 the provinces of Havana and City of Havana. Now *I was the one* who had administrative tasks to fulfill. I was there a little over a year, and then was assigned to the agriculture department of the party Central Committee.

The Ministry of Agriculture has an agriculture section and a livestock section. The agriculture section deals with the production of vegetables, fruit, and so on. The livestock section has responsibility for the production of beef and milk, as well as everything related to cattle, horses, pigs, and poultry—all of it.

The Central Committee's Agriculture Department oversees

the entire work of the Ministry of Agriculture—both agriculture and livestock. That's what I did from 1972 until late 1975, when I first went to Angola.

WATERS: You were also provincial party secretary in Las Tunas for a time, weren't you?

ZAYAS: Yes. In January 1980 Fidel sent me to Las Tunas as party secretary, and I was there for five years, until 1985.

WATERS: Why Las Tunas?

ZAYAS: In comparison to the other provinces, Las Tunas was one of the most backward. The fact that I'm from there was important. They needed someone who knew the province.

WATERS: Why was Las Tunas more backward than other provinces?

ZAYAS: For one thing, there was no momentum within the administrative bodies to try to solve the problems of development in the province, because nothing was done without consulting the party.

When you make the decisions on what you need to do, you work better. You work with enthusiasm. Fidel explained this problem of overcentralization to me and said it needed to change. The first thing I did was meet with all the leaders in Las Tunas and tell them that each of them was responsible for their own work. The only thing prohibited was "inflating balloons"—an expression we use that means "telling lies."

If anyone blows up a balloon for me, I said, I'll prick it and let out the air. We gave everyone the space to develop their area of responsibility, to take the steps necessary.

If you pay attention to people, talk to them, pose problems and concerns, and ask for the help you need, people respond.

I'll give you an example of the challenges we faced. There was just one small asphalt plant in Las Tunas. It was in the provincial capital, with another under construction in Puerto Padre. The plant we had didn't produce enough to meet our needs—not even enough to fill potholes. Plus many of the streets were only dirt roads. What's more, we couldn't transport the asphalt more than twenty kilometers, since it cools and compacts.

In the five years I was there, we built four asphalt plants. This made it possible to pave roads and improve the highway.

The president of People's Power, the municipal government body, told the local Committees in Defense of the Revolution, the CDRs, and residents in the neighborhoods: If you'll build the sidewalk and curb, we'll make sure there's asphalt for the street. It was done by the people.

To take another example, there's a municipality called Colombia that used to be part of Camagüey. It's near Guáimaro, a town close to the border between Camagüey and Las Tunas. Only the main road through the center of town was paved. And Colombia is a big town, with a sugar mill. So we paved all the side streets off the main road, some seventeen kilometers in all.

Housing was another problem in Las Tunas. I did a calculation. At the rate they were building housing for the families of workers there, it would have taken ninety-nine years to solve the problem. So we came up with a plan to solve it in fifteen or twenty years. In the five years I was in Las Tunas, we built thirty thousand housing units. The municipal government would sell workers the materials, and they'd get a crew together and organize voluntary labor to build their own houses. On weekends they'd be lent a crane to put the roofs in place. They'd do two or three roofs in a weekend. In other words, you look for a solution, a way, so people can transform their lives.

The party helped get this going. A brigade was sent to the Siguaney cement factory in Sancti Spíritus province to get cement, which was then sold to the workers. Camagüey gave us a plant to produce sand that had previously been in Guáimaro. A rock crusher in Camagüey was donated to Las Tunas by the Ministry of Construction. We built asphalt plants, as I mentioned earlier, and the brick factory was expanded to produce bricks needed to build walls.

WATERS: You seem to be describing something similar to what was done on a national level, starting with the rectification process initiated following the first session of the party congress in 1986. That's when the minibrigades became a movement—teams of workers organized through their workplaces who volunteered to build apartment buildings, childcare centers, and other social projects.[4]

ZAYAS: What we did was a little different. There was a time when a big push was made to use minibrigades to find a solution to the housing problem. Each entity came up with a plan to build housing for its workers, and the minibrigades were created.

The state construction contingents primarily built large buildings. The prevailing notion at the time was that housing had to be built in the form of apartment buildings. This was the early 1980s. But I said to Fidel, "Look, putting up apartment buildings is fine for Havana, where land is tight and there isn't sufficient space. But here in Las Tunas land is plentiful. It's not necessary to limit housing construction to apartment buildings."

So what people began building in Las Tunas were not only apartment buildings, but one- and two-story houses as well. The people who needed houses got together them-

---

4. See glossary, Rectification process.

selves. Work was done in their free time, usually Saturdays and Sundays.

The municipal government and the CDRs organized distribution of materials and resources in each neighborhood. The CDR knew who was having problems building their houses. They made up a list, and using this list they'd tell people: "Go and get two sacks of cement." Or "Go get a cubic meter of sand." The state sold it to them at a very low price.

WATERS: Looking back on it, how would you assess the time you were in Las Tunas?

ZAYAS: We met the goals set out in the plan. We surpassed our sugar quota, which hadn't been reached in years. The cattle herds grew. We increased the output of vegetables and grain, as well as eggs, poultry, pork, and many other things. For this we won the emulation contest for July 26, 1981. Being the province with the best results, we had the honor of hosting the national July 26 celebration.

WATERS: From 1978 to 1980, and from 1987 to 1998, you had responsibilities for leading the Youth Army of Labor, the EJT. Where did the EJT come from and what does it do?

ZAYAS: The origins of the Youth Army of Labor date back to 1968. It came out of the need for a labor force in agriculture.

First came the columns led principally by the Union of Young Communists. The first of these was in Camagüey, initially called the Centennial Youth Column. Many young people joined it. The name "Centennial" was a symbol of the struggle—1968 was the hundredth anniversary of the beginning of Cuba's independence war.

Later the Centennial Youth Column was transformed into a labor force for other areas as well—not just agriculture. In 1973 the Youth Army of Labor was founded, led by the FAR, the Revolutionary Armed Forces of Cuba.

III. SOLDIER OF THE REVOLUTION

The EJT had two objectives.

First, drawn from youth called to military service, it provided a much-needed labor force.

Second, these young people were at the same time trained for defense, since we've always been threatened by imperialist aggression. The youth columns were no longer just in Camagüey, which is in the plains. They also trained in the mountains. The EJT units receive training for any contingency. They provide a force that's able to fight, resist, and produce.

The EJT's structure is the same as that of the regular armed forces. But the state budget does not have to provide for it. They cover their costs by what they produce.

The Youth Army of Labor has helped solve major labor shortages in sugar, coffee, and citrus production. It also helped construct the central railway. Initially it built schools and housing in the countryside as well.

WATERS: Military service is obligatory for all young men, isn't it?

ZAYAS: Yes, for two years. Military service must be fulfilled, either in the regular armed forces—the FAR or the Ministry of Interior—or in the Youth Army of Labor.

WATERS: How is it decided who joins the EJT and who joins the Revolutionary Armed Forces or the Ministry of Interior?

ZAYAS: Some have personal preferences. And we always take into account that some young people come from families that face greater economic difficulties.

Youth joining the EJT are often from the countryside. They've already acquired work habits, or were working to help support their families. These are not marginalized youth, not at all. They are the children of workers. After they've completed their service, they can choose to stay in the army and go on to one of the military schools. That's their decision. Many FAR officers came out of the EJT, including some generals.

Any young person with a high school diploma who completes a year and a half of military service can choose to continue their studies, whether or not they graduated from a preuniversity high school, and without having to pass other exams. They can take advantage of what we call Order 18, issued by the minister of the FAR, which allows these young people to enter the university if they so choose.

The Youth Army of Labor was in Angola too. During the last stage of the war, in 1988, the EJT helped build the airport in the south of Angola, in record time, which was decisive to the victory there.[5]

WATERS: The crisis known as the Special Period—which began in the early 1990s following the disintegration of the regimes of Eastern Europe and the Soviet Union—led to serious food shortages.[6] Many people have told us that the EJT's contribution to overcoming this crisis was indispensable. Even today, we're told the Youth Army of Labor brings large quantities of food into the cities and sells at prices below those at other markets. How is this done?

ZAYAS: The EJT organizes agricultural markets, under the direction of the FAR. What the EJT produces is brought in to be sold at prices lower than those offered by private farmers or middlemen.

WATERS: What's the reason for this?

ZAYAS: To help the population, and to keep prices down in other markets, including those organized under the responsibility of the Ministry of Agriculture. The EJT sells at prices significantly lower than the cap set by the state. But the EJT

---

5. See part IV, "Defending Angola's Sovereignty."
6. See glossary, Special Period.

III. SOLDIER OF THE REVOLUTION

> We cannot forget that [with the Special Period] we were faced with confronting and solving practically insoluble problems. How were we to do that? How, when the country was left on its own, losing everything overnight: markets, raw materials, fertilizers, fuel, credits; and also blockaded, and on top of that, morally battered, because it was a very hard blow for all of us to see those who had been our allies in the struggle collapsing. . . .
>
> We have recovered so much morally, politically, in terms of consciousness, from that crushing blow we received five or six years ago; it has been demonstrated that our country, like a boxer, has a very tough jaw, it's impossible to knock us down. We resisted, we withstood the ideological blow and were able to heroically withstand the tremendous material blow we received. . . .
>
> One day we may have to erect a monument to the Special Period! If we keep on learning the way we have been learning . . . we will have to start laying the cornerstone for a monument to the Special Period, for teaching us to live off our own resources and to take much better advantage of everything we have, that invaluable treasure which is our people's intelligence, knowledge, and preparation.
>
> FIDEL CASTRO
> APRIL 30, 1996[*]

---

[*] Fidel Castro, Speech at closing session of seventeenth congress of Central Organization of Cuban Trade Unions, in *Granma International*, May 15, 1996. An English translation is available online at http://lanic.utexas.edu/project/castro/db/1996/19960501.html.

markets still generate a surplus; they don't lose money. So workers want to go where the EJT is selling.

The Youth Army of Labor also initiated the Sunday agricultural fairs. That's an EJT initiative to help people with lower income and fewer resources especially. "What I spent buying from the EJT would have bought only half as much elsewhere," people sometimes say.

Many of these policies were established by Rigoberto García, then a division general, who headed the EJT for thirty years. He was a strong defender of working people who shop at EJT markets. If an older person was short on money, the policy Rigoberto established was, "Give it to them. No charge." That's the kind of person he is, and that's the way he ran the EJT markets.

KOPPEL: We've been told the EJT plays a big role in citrus production.

ZAYAS: That's true, an extremely important role. Take the example of the very large Jagüey Grande citrus enterprise in Matanzas. During the Special Period production shrank due to a lack of resources and a shortage of labor in the region. The Youth Army of Labor was asked to take over that whole operation. Some six thousand EJT cadres went to work there to reverse the losses, and citrus production began growing again.

What's being done now in the citrus industry is based on experience gained by the Youth Army of Labor in organizing work and organizing wages based on productivity. When workers produce more, instead of raising the rate, they get paid more. These incentives have translated into more work getting done by a smaller workforce, so the Youth Army of Labor wasn't needed any longer. The civilian work force in the citrus-growing area was sufficient to raise production to half a million tons a year. Previously it had never gone much above two hundred thousand tons.

Under capitalism, when you work harder and produce more, the boss gets more surplus value. Here it's the workers who gain. That's what the Cuban Revolution changed almost half a century ago.

WATERS: You left the Youth Army of Labor in 1998. What did you do then?

ZAYAS: In 1998 I retired from active duty in the armed forces. We'd reduced the number of active units, and it was important to open up space for young officers. Two years later I was asked to become part of the national leadership of the Association of Combatants of the Cuban Revolution. That's where I've been ever since.

Central to the work of the Combatants Association is imparting the history and lessons of some five decades of revolutionary struggle to new generations. This is part of our collective political consciousness, of our capacity to resist and survive, of workers' capacity to do so. This is what made it possible for us to withstand the Special Period.

Had the workers not been conscious here, we wouldn't have survived.

This is especially true in the eastern provinces, where there have always been fewer resources than in Havana. Nonetheless there's more consciousness.

Much of what's been accomplished is due to the work done by the party leadership over the years since the victory of the revolution—work leading the broad masses to understand the reason for problems we face and measures we've taken.

This has always been Fidel's strength; he's had a very clear vision. Whenever a problem has arisen, he's always been on the front lines, leading, explaining. Whenever we've thought some problem couldn't be solved, Fidel led us to find the solution.

This is very important in understanding how the Cuban

> Tomorrow's leaders must never forget that this is a revolution of the poor and humble, by the poor and humble, and for the poor and humble. Never let the enemy's siren songs make you go soft. Always be aware that the enemy, by its very nature, will never stop being aggressive, domineering, and treacherous. Never separate yourselves from our workers, peasants, and the rest of the people. . . .
>
> It is the responsibility of the historic leadership of the revolution to prepare the new generations to take on the enormous responsibility of continuing forward with the revolutionary process.
>
> RAÚL CASTRO
> JANUARY 1, 2009[*]

people have resisted all these years, and how we survived the debacle of the Soviet Union. We were all alone here. Yet we were able to resist, and we continue to resist.

The Cuban Revolution proves that it's possible in today's world to make a revolution just ninety miles from the strongest and most ferocious imperialist power on earth. Cuba provides an example to the peoples of the Americas and the world that revolution is possible, that working people can struggle and win.

---

[*] Raúl Castro, Speech at Rally Celebrating Fiftieth Anniversary of the Cuban Revolution. An English translation is available online at http://www.juventudrebelde.co.cu/2009-01-02/raul-castro-speech-on-the-50th-anniversary-of-the-revolution/.

PART IV

Defending Angola's Sovereignty

IV. Defending Angola's Sovereignty

Between November 1975 and May 1991, more than 375,000 members of Cuba's Revolutionary Armed Forces volunteered for service in Angola in response to requests for help from the government of that country in turning back two major invasions by South Africa's apartheid regime. An additional 50,000 internationalist volunteers served in civilian posts. The South African army's unrelenting aggression over a fourteen-year time span was carried out in alliance with counterrevolutionary Angolan groups and received substantial US financial, military, and diplomatic support. But the white supremacist invaders and their backers were defeated.

As recounted in these pages, beginning in 1975 Alfonso Zayas served three tours as part of this internationalist effort in the 1970s and '80s.

Cuba's active support to the independence struggle in Africa's Portuguese colonies had begun more than a decade earlier. In early 1965 Ernesto Che Guevara made a tour of Africa, during which he met with leaders of the national liberation struggles in Angola, Mozambique, Guinea-Bissau, and Cape Verde and pledged Cuba's full support to their struggle to overturn rule by Lisbon. A few months later Guevara himself led a six-month mission of 128 Cuban combatants to the former Belgian colony of the Congo to assist anti-imperialist forces there.

Over the next ten years, Cuban advisers and trainers aided the movements in Portugal's African colonies. With the fall of the Portuguese dictatorship in 1974—accelerated by the impact of spreading armed liberation struggles—the former colonies were granted their independence. Angola was to become independent on November 11, 1975, with a government led by the MPLA (Popular Movement for the Liberation of Angola), the strongest liberation movement in the country.

To prevent that from occurring, the army of apartheid South Africa invaded Angola. The invasion was supported by Washington and aided by the proimperialist government of Zaire.[1] Among other things, the regime of president Mobutu Sese Seko in Zaire hoped to annex oil-rich Cabinda province.

The goal of the South African and US rulers was to block the MPLA from forming the new government and instead to hand over power to their allies in UNITA (National Union for the Total Independence of Angola), led by Jonas Savimbi, and the FNLA (National Front for the Liberation of Angola), led by Holden Roberto. By early November, the South African forces and their allies were closing in on the capital city of Luanda.

Cuba's response to an appeal from Angola's new president, Agostinho Neto, for combat forces to help prevent South African forces from taking Luanda is described by Colombian novelist Gabriel García Márquez, based on extensive interviews with Cuban leaders. "The leadership of the Communist Party of Cuba did not have more than twenty-four hours to make the decision," he wrote in 1977, "and it did so, without vacillation, on November 5. . . . That decision was an independent and sover-

1. Two countries historically share the name Congo. Congo-Brazzaville (formally, Republic of the Congo), north of Angola, won independence from France in 1960. The Congo (Democratic Republic of the Congo, known as Zaire from 1971 to 1997), northeast of Angola, won independence from Belgium in 1960.

IV. DEFENDING ANGOLA'S SOVEREIGNTY

eign act of Cuba, and it was only after it was taken, and not before, that the Soviet Union was notified."[2]

The mission was named Operation Carlota, after a slave woman from the Triunvirato sugar mill in Cuba who, armed with a machete, led a slave rebellion in 1843 that extended over a number of plantations in Matanzas province. Known as "Black Carlota," she was captured and drawn and quartered by the Spanish colonial troops.

As Zayas describes here, the Cuban internationalists were decisive in halting the invading forces a few kilometers outside Luanda, a matter of hours before the independence ceremony. They then helped lead a counteroffensive both to the north and to the south. By March 27, 1976, "when the last South African soldiers crossed the Namibian border after a retreat of more than seven hundred kilometers, one of the most brilliant pages in the liberation of Black Africa had been written," said Fidel Castro on April 19, 1976.[3]

Tens of thousands in Cuba had volunteered to be part of this effort. "The immense majority went to Angola in the full conviction that they were carrying out an act of political solidarity, with the same consciousness and courage with which fifteen years earlier they had defeated the invasion at Playa Girón," García Márquez wrote. "That is why Operation Carlota was not a simple expedition of professional soldiers, but a popular war."[4]

After being driven back across the border, the apartheid re-

---

2. Gabriel García Márquez, "Cuba in Angola: Operation Carlota," in Fidel Castro, *Cuba's Internationalist Foreign Policy 1975–80* (Pathfinder, 1981) pp. 421–22 [2010 printing].
3. Fidel Castro, "Angola: African Girón," in *Cuba's Internationalist Foreign Policy*, p. 110.
4. García Márquez, "Cuba in Angola," p. 425.

gime in South Africa, with backing and aid from the US government, helped initiate a bloody counterrevolutionary war against the new Angolan government—a war waged primarily by UNITA. UNITA's operations inside Angola received ample cross-border support from South African forces based in Namibia, then under South African rule, including further incursions by the apartheid regime. Faced with this situation, Angola requested that Cuba maintain its internationalist military mission in order to forestall other South African invasions. Over the next decade of stalemate, the war cost hundreds of thousands of Angolans their lives.

The stalemate lasted until late 1987 when, in response to another full-scale South African invasion, the Cuban revolutionary leadership moved rapidly and decisively to reinforce Cuba's military in Angola.

The decisive battle to block the advancing South African forces was fought at the town of Cuito Cuanavale in southeastern Angola, where a group of Angolan and Cuban troops were surrounded. Over several months the town's defenders, led by the Cubans, repulsed repeated South African thrusts. Meanwhile, Cuban and Angolan reinforcements moved toward Cuito Cuanavale and other units simultaneously mounted a flanking operation in a broad arc southward toward Namibia. By March 1988 South African positions themselves were being threatened. Recognizing they could not take Cuito Cuanavale, the apartheid forces began a full-scale retreat toward the Namibian border.

Faced with growing mass struggles against apartheid rule at home as well, the South African regime sued for peace. In December 1988 an agreement was signed at the United Nations in New York between Angola, Cuba, and South Africa, in the presence of representatives of the US government. The accords called on South Africa to withdraw its forces from Angola and to recognize Namibia's independence. Immediately following the signing of this agreement, Cuba and Angola jointly agreed to the withdrawal of Cuban forces.

The last Cuban troops left Angola in May 1991. Some two thousand Cuban internationalists had given their lives in the nearly sixteen-year mission.

"The crushing defeat of the racist army at Cuito Cuanavale was a victory for the whole of Africa!" said Nelson Mandela during a visit to Cuba in July 1991. Expressing the gratitude of the people of South Africa, Mandela underscored the contribution of the Cuban people to the overthrow of the apartheid regime itself. Cuito Cuanavale, he said, was "a turning point in the struggle to free the continent and our country from the scourge of apartheid!"[5]

WATERS: You volunteered for Cuba's internationalist mission in Angola three times—at three different times, with different responsibilities. Start from the beginning. How did Cuba's aid to Angola begin and what were its aims?

ZAYAS: I first arrived in Angola in early December 1975. At that point, South African forces, backed by Washington, were just three hundred kilometers from the capital city of Luanda, coming from the south. They were advancing along a line extending from Porto Amboim to Quibala. They had a powerful force, with armored vehicles, artillery, planes, and infantry.

Approaching Luanda from the north, with another powerful force, was the FNLA, led by Holden Roberto, backed by the Zairian and US governments. They had been stopped just

5. Nelson Mandela, "We Will Ensure that the Poor and Rightless Will Rule the Land of Their Birth," in Nelson Mandela and Fidel Castro, *How Far We Slaves Have Come!* (Pathfinder, 1991), pp. 22–23 [2009 printing].

Angola

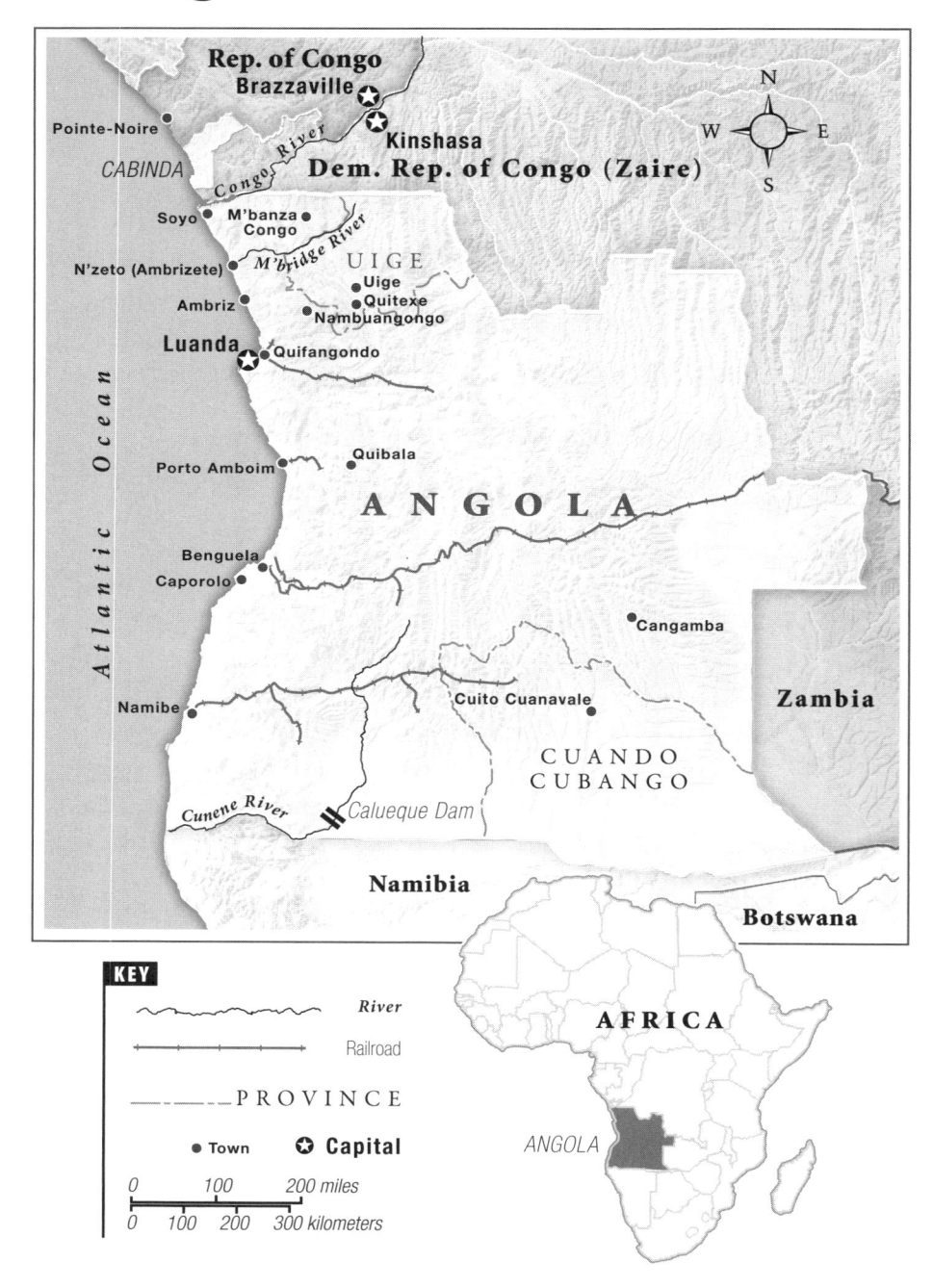

twenty kilometers away, in Quifangondo. They were practically at the gates of the capital.

And then there were the forces of UNITA, led by Jonas Savimbi. UNITA had the political and military support of the South Africans and Washington, which gave them weaponry and supplies of all types.

In response to this dire situation, Agostinho Neto, the president of Angola and leader of the MPLA, asked for Cuba's help. Cuba had supported the MPLA since 1965, when the guerrilla struggle against the Portuguese was in its early stages. If Neto had not requested Cuba's help, or if the Cuban forces hadn't arrived in time, the South African military would have captured Luanda. UNITA and Savimbi, or the FNLA and Holden Roberto, would have been installed as the government, thwarting the independence struggle of the Angolan people.

The people of Luanda supported the MPLA, which had led the struggle against Portuguese colonialism. But the MPLA did not have the organization or the means to stabilize the city's defense. It found itself in a corner.

With the support of the Cuban volunteers, the Angolan army—FAPLA, the Popular Armed Forces for the Liberation of Angola—turned them back.

KOPPEL: What were your responsibilities?

ZAYAS: I arrived in Angola in December 1975 to work with Jorge Risquet, assisting Agostinho Neto in the work of the party and government.

But that changed. As a result of the military situation, Angolan and Cuban troops were launching an offensive toward the north—toward a spot on the border with Zaire then called San Antonio do Zaire, today Soyo.

Close to midnight on December 31, we were meeting at the headquarters of the Cuban military mission to analyze this

> On October 14, 1975, a mortal danger hovered over Angola. A powerful South African armored column penetrated the country and began a rapid advance towards the north in the direction of Luanda. They encountered the first resistance in Caporolo on November 2, organized by an infantry force made up of Angolans and Cuban advisers from the Benguela training center to the south. In this action, the enemy lost four armored units and suffered considerable losses, but given their superiority they were able to continue their march. In the battle, four Cubans were killed and several were wounded or missing; the Angolan loses were more numerous. The blood of our two peoples fused into the African earth.
>
> On November 4, in Cuba—upon learning the news—the leadership of the country, headed by the commander-in-chief, made the historic decision to send the first combat units to Angola. A battalion of special troops were sent by air and an artillery regiment by sea. Operation Carlota had begun.
>
> JORGE RISQUET
> 2004[*]

offensive operation. An officer was needed to coordinate actions between the Angolan forces—those of the FAPLA—and the Cuban forces that were there to give them support. I volunteered. Abelardo Colomé—Furry, as we know him—was the head of the Cuban military mission in Angola. Since I was working under Risquet, Colomé told me I could go if Risquet authorized it, and he did.

[*] Jorge Risquet, "Two Centuries of Solidarity: The Deep Roots of Cuba's Internationalism," in *Tricontinental*, no. 158, 2004.

That was around 1:00 a.m. By 4:30 a.m. I was on my way.

Risquet told me there were two compañeros who'd been with him earlier in Africa and would help me with anything.[6] I picked them up in a Cuban jeep and off we went, together with a driver and someone else in my escort. There were five of us. By later in the day we'd caught up with the Angolan force supported by Cuban tanks and artillery.

These troops had fought a battle against the FNLA and Zairian forces in Nambuangongo, some fifty kilometers north of Luanda. After the clash they had pulled back, and that's where we met up with them. Together we continued on, trying to get to Uíge province, then called Carmona. That's where Holden Roberto and the FNLA general staff were. We had to take a long roundabout route, since all the bridges along the coast had been blown up by the enemy. We maneuvered along some hills, by way of the road from Luanda to Carmona.

There were small groups of the FNLA in all the villages we passed through. But when they heard the artillery and tanks we were bringing, they fled. The FAPLA Ninth Brigade, which was with us, had a company of soldiers who'd formerly been commandos in the Portuguese army and fought very well. They were traveling in vans with the seats facing outward. When they arrived in those villages, they'd jump out from both sides and advance. Any remaining FNLA forces would flee.

6. From August 1965 to January 1967, Risquet headed a contingent of Cuban internationalist combatants in the former French colony of Congo-Brazzaville. Known as Column 2, this detachment was originally conceived as a support unit for Column 1, led by Ernesto Che Guevara, which was working to assist liberation forces in the former Belgian colony of the Congo. Risquet and the leadership of Column 2 were given responsibility for initiating collaboration with and aid to the MPLA.

One of the little villages along the highway was Quitexe. It was said that two FNLA companies were there, along with a company of white mercenaries from Portugal and other countries.[7] In that village heavier combat took place. The battle lasted several hours, with the FNLA forces suffering a number of casualties.

After we took Quitexe, we continued on to Carmona, a town about two hundred kilometers from the coast. When we got there, it had already been taken by another FAPLA column coming from the other direction and led by Commander Víctor Schueg Colás, a Cuban. After a fight, the FNLA had retreated toward the north.

We then headed west in the direction of Ambrizete—today it's called N'zeto—and Ambriz, two small villages along the coast. Between Carmona and Ambrizete, the Portuguese had built an immense dirt landing strip, which NATO had been allowed to use as well. The FNLA had forces in a little village there, supported by a company of white mercenaries. We fought them and took the village and airstrip, including warehouses full of weapons and ammunition, as well as nine very large napalm bombs. A mechanized battalion that Fidel had sent to support Schueg's column joined us there and continued on with us to Ambrizete.

The enemy forces in Ambrizete were supported by a company of white mercenaries, plus some Koreans who were experts in blowing up bridges. As the enemy retreated over a very long and high bridge spanning the fast-flowing Mbridge River, they blew it up. We were unable to cross and had to

7. Describing the conduct of these mercenaries and the FNLA forces toward the Angolan population, the January 30, 1976, *New York Times* said: "Refugees report that these towns. . . have been completely sacked and that their populations have fled. . . . The Zaire army units were said to have been the most active in the looting."

IV. DEFENDING ANGOLA'S SOVEREIGNTY

wait for a raft to be brought up from the south. We couldn't move all the military equipment for about two weeks, when they brought a *changada*, which is a barge with two engines.

By that time Schueg had arrived at San Salvador province—today it's M'banza Congo. This is Angola's northernmost province, except for Cabinda. It's on the border with Zaire. The FNLA leadership was still in that region, along with about forty or fifty white mercenaries. A number of mercenaries were killed, and Callan, their main leader, was captured. Later he was tried and executed.[8] We continued ahead from the south, along the coast, to San Antonio do Zaire. There one mercenary died in combat and their second in command, John Baker, was captured.

We left Luanda on December 31, 1975, and reached the banks of the Congo River, dividing Zaire from Angola, more than a month later, on February 7, 1976. We celebrated the liberation of the north with a flag-raising ceremony attended by four members of the MPLA Political Bureau, including Lúcio Lara and Iko Carreira. My ten days had turned into almost six weeks.

After that I stayed on to train the Angolans, so we could turn over to them the tanks, artillery, and BM-21 rocket launchers we'd brought. In April 1976 all the equipment was handed over to the Angolans.

I then returned to Luanda to help organize a parade to commemorate the anniversary of the establishment of the Angolan armed forces on August 2, 1974. There had never before been a parade on that scale in Luanda.

---

8. "Colonel Callan"—not, in fact, a colonel—was a Cypriot named Costas Georgiou who had been a British paratrooper dishonorably discharged and jailed for robbing a post office in Northern Ireland.

COURTESY ALFONSO ZAYAS

The US government never imagined Cuba could send tens of thousands of armed volunteers to help the Angolan people defeat invasion by South Africa's apartheid regime, Zayas says. "Washington's great strategists couldn't even conceive of the kind of consciousness the Cubans demonstrated."

Above, Alfonso Zayas (left) on plane with Angolan military leaders, including João Luís Neto (right), vice minister of armed forces, known by his nom de guerre, Cheto, 1976. Zayas served three tours of duty in Angola, 1976, 1977, and 1985–87.

At the end of 1976 I returned to Cuba.

WATERS: After the success of the operation in the north in early 1976, did this part of Angola remain under government control, or were there other battles in this region later?

ZAYAS: At that time, in 1976, the north was considered liberated. It was in the hands of the MPLA. That's why Holden Roberto left Angola and went to Zaire. He was in the pay of the CIA and lived in Zaire, where he was married to a sister-in-law of dictator Mobutu Sese Seko. Later there were other complications, and the fighting continued.

KOPPEL: What about the charge that Cuba was intervening in an internal struggle among Angolans?

ZAYAS: It's true there was a conflict between different organizations in Angola: the FNLA, the MPLA, UNITA, the FLEC—the Cabinda Enclave Liberation Front. But the Cubans didn't interfere in it.

In part the divisions were regional, based on tribe. In the northern region, people generally supported the FNLA. In the southern areas, people supported UNITA. And in the central region they supported the MPLA. In Cabinda, people were with FLEC.

But what was really involved? UNITA and the FNLA were backed by Zaire, the South Africans, and the US government. So it was no longer just a struggle among Angolans. What was involved was imperialist intervention to thwart Angolan independence and take control of Angola as the Portuguese withdrew.

As for the Cubans, we were defending Angola from aggression by South Africa above all, but also by Zaire—both backed by Washington. We didn't get involved in the internal struggle among these organizations. That was a problem among Angolans. It was something for them to resolve.

WATERS: When did you return to Angola?

> Angola is a territory rich in natural resources. Cabinda, one of its provinces, has large oil deposits. This country has great mineral wealth—diamonds, copper, iron. This is one of the reasons why the imperialists want to take hold of Angola. . . .
> When the Angolan people were about to attain independence—just as Guinea-Bissau, Mozambique, Cape Verde, and other countries attained their independence—imperialism worked out a way to crush the revolutionary movement. And to carry out this scheme, the US government launched South African troops against Angola. . . .
> Thus Angola was being threatened on the north by the FNLA and was attacked on the south by regular troops organized into armored columns. Everything was ready to take control of Angola before November 11. And the plan was solid; the only thing was that it failed. They had not counted on international solidarity, on the support given to the heroic people of Angola by the socialist countries, in the first place, and by the revolutionary movements and progressive governments of Africa, or the support we Cubans, among the world's progressive governments, also gave Angola. . . .
> That is, the heroic struggle of the Angolan people, supported by the international revolutionary movement, has made the imperialist plan fail.
>
> FIDEL CASTRO
> DECEMBER 22, 1975[*]

[*] Fidel Castro, "Closing Speech to First Party Congress," in *Cuba's Internationalist Foreign Policy*, pp. 97–99.

ZAYAS: As I said, I came back to Cuba in late 1976. But in early 1977, after I'd been in Cuba about two months, Risquet asked me to return to Angola.

At Angola's request, Cuba was stepping up collaboration on all levels at that time. Cubans were helping in education, in construction, in public health—in every area. By 1977 there were about three thousand Cuban civilians working in Angola, in sixteen of Angola's eighteen provinces.

So we created a central leadership structure of the Cuban personnel in Angola, both on a national level and in the provinces. That's what Risquet asked me to help with. I was basically second-in-command to Risquet for everything involving the civilian missions—supplies, relations with the Angolan government, and so on.

For this I had to visit all the provinces. I went as far south as Cuando Cubango—which is two and a half hours by plane—to take supplies and to establish the mission there. Ten or twelve compañeros were going to work in that province, which was UNITA's stronghold. That's the region where the battles in Cangamba and Cuito Cuanavale took place later in the war.[9] UNITA came to have a powerful army there, backed by the South Africans and with the support of US imperialism.

On May 27, 1977, a few months after I arrived for my second tour, there was an attempted coup against the leadership of President Neto. Nito Alves was the leader of that counterrevolutionary uprising.

Alves was Angola's minister of the interior. His influence extended throughout practically the entire country, since he

9. Cangamba was the scene of a seven-day battle in August 1983 in which some eight hundred FAPLA and Cuban combatants, without food or water, battled more than three thousand UNITA troops and dealt them a decisive defeat. For Cuito Cuanavale, see pages 132–33.

appointed the provincial commissioners, who were in fact the government in the provinces. Alves had the support of the people he'd appointed. At one point, it was not the MPLA that was governing but Alves's faction within the MPLA— the "microfaction," as it became known.

Several members of the MPLA Political Bureau were involved. These included Monstruo Inmortal [Immortal Monster]. His real name was Jacobo Caetano. He was a member of the Political Bureau, FAPLA's chief of operations, and practically Neto's right-hand man. There was also Bakaloff—Eduardo Evaristo—who was FAPLA's political head.

In other words, the counterrevolutionary coup leaders included FAPLA's political head, its chief of operations, the minister of the interior, several other ministers, and nearly all the commissioners in every province.

What happened?

Alves's forces took over the government radio station in Luanda. That station played a decisive role, since it was one of the few sources of information and people followed it closely. Its broadcasts from Luanda were rebroadcast and networked to all the provincial radio stations. The microfaction began attacking the MPLA over the air. That was the beginning of the action.

They put a Pioneer on the air to speak.[10] Actually, he wasn't a Pioneer, but he was young and that's how they presented him. They'd given him a piece of propaganda criticizing Neto to read aloud, which he did. Until then they'd criticized the MPLA but said nothing about Neto.

The radio station called on people to go to the presidential palace, the seat of government. And people headed there.

10. The Pioneers was a children's organization set up by the MPLA in 1975.

KOPPEL: What was the response of Cubans there collaborating with the Angolan government?

ZAYAS: The Cubans didn't know who was who, or what was what. But there were Cubans in each of the provinces, and the heads of our civilian missions knew the problems there. They had good relations with the provincial commissioners, with the FAPLA, with the Ministry of the Interior, with the security forces.

When the Cubans working in each province heard what was happening, they immediately said, "No way!" One of these was Rafael Moracén, the Cuban adviser to the commander of Neto's presidential regiment. When coup supporters heeded the call over the radio to go to the presidential palace, they were met by this regiment, which turned them back.

Moracén, with Angolan and Cuban forces in tanks, then headed to the radio station. Having taken the station, the microfaction practically had power in its hands, since they could issue directions heard everywhere. But Moracén's brigade retook the station.

I was at the Hotel Presidente at the time, recording the radio broadcasts. "What's going on here?" you could hear Moracén saying when he arrived at the station. "You there, what are you saying about Neto? Neto is the president here!" You could hear his voice: "Neto is the president here!" That's what Moracén said.

After the radio station was retaken, things calmed down.

A decisive role was played by those heading the Cuban civilian mission in each province, along with the Cuban armed forces there. They kept the situation under control. We had great influence at every level, beginning with Neto, who was very appreciative of the aid provided by the Cubans. And we had influence in the provinces, too. Because of the role we'd played in defeating the South African invasion, Cuban collaboration was accepted. When asked for advice, we gave it. We voiced our opinions—very tactfully—and the Angolans we worked with were quite receptive.

WATERS: What were the differences between the Neto leadership and the microfaction? What was behind the coup attempt?

ZAYAS: Lust for power and riches. Angola has oil, it has gold, diamonds, everything. It's a country with immense mineral wealth.

WATERS: Fidel has talked about the differences between Cuban and Soviet advisers in Angola. What was your experience?

ZAYAS: The Soviets had some advisers in Angola, although not many. They had a different strategic military conception from ours. The Soviets favored big armies. What was needed in Angola, however, wasn't big armies or grand military strategies. The help they needed was much more practical.

The Soviets did give a lot of support in weaponry and equipment. It was for Angola, but it was handled by the Cubans. Why? Because few Angolans knew how to use most of it. They had to be trained. Plus the Soviets had experienced setbacks in Africa before, where they'd sent arms and support that had been lost to the enemy or abandoned. That's why the Soviet weaponry was handled by the Cuban force.

Many Angolan technicians and armed forces personnel were trained here in Cuba. The Soviets also provided training to the Angolans—to pilots, combat engineers, communications personnel, and so on—teaching them to use the equipment. They trained a lot of Angolan military personnel in Russia. But the Angolans generally accepted the Cuban advisers more readily than the Soviet ones. They understood our advice better, since it was more practical, more in tune with the needs and character of the struggle in Africa.

IV. DEFENDING ANGOLA'S SOVEREIGNTY

WATERS: What about Fidel's role in leading the Angola operation?

ZAYAS: Using a map of Angola, Fidel led the war as if it were here in Cuba. He knew what was happening in every little corner of the country. He received information every day from those of us who were over there and from his liaisons, who would come and go.

Sometimes Fidel knew things you wouldn't even imagine, and he'd give instructions for what had to be done. "Do this, do that, because the South Africans are going to do such-and-such." And he'd be right. Fidel directed the battle of Cuito Cuanavale against the South Africans, as if he were in the forward command post in Angola.

The big decisions to send forces to Angola were made by Fidel. The US government never imagined Cuba could send fifty thousand armed men to fight in Africa. How could Cuba do so, since we had no transatlantic merchant ships set up for troop transport, nor did Angola? But we Cubans, of course, are prepared for the greatest sacrifices, and that's how our forces were able to be sent to Angola. All of Washington's great strategists couldn't even conceive of that.

How was it possible to send thousands of men aboard aged turboprop passenger planes and merchant ships? Onboard the freighters, they had to travel in the cargo hold. The men couldn't go on deck or they'd be spotted. But then how do they relieve themselves? How do they bathe and wash up? How do they eat, since the ship wasn't set up to provide meals for thousands of men? To spend three weeks like that, who can bear it? You need to have the kind of consciousness the Cubans who went had.

Their spirits were high, because they had confidence in Fidel. Fidel tried to meet with every group of soldiers that left. He'd go and talk to them. He'd explain what the situation was.

And if he couldn't go himself, he'd send someone else.

Only with a leadership like Fidel's could something like that be achieved.

Our forces arrived in Angola in November 1975, right when they were needed. It was the same in 1987, with those needed during the siege of Cuito Cuanavale. Because in both cases, there was no force in Angola capable of taking on the advancing South African troops. Fidel made the decision to send what was needed to win, and they arrived in time to achieve that.

Fidel led everything that had to be done to defeat the South African forces. He'd spend entire nights analyzing and figuring out what had to be done and how. His direct participation was decisive.

KOPPEL: What about the civilian mission you were helping to lead?

ZAYAS: By the time I left Angola in 1978, there were, as I said, more than three thousand Cuban civilian collaborators. Most were in health and education, although there were some in every sector.

WATERS: How long would they volunteer for?

ZAYAS: They'd generally go for two years. Some went for one year, but most often two. I'm talking about the civilians. Soldiers also went for two years, but they stayed longer if they had to. The soldiers were volunteers too, but they acted under orders. The civilians committed to two years and after that went home. There was a rotation to send replacements.

The civilian volunteers got one month of vacation each year, in Cuba. That involved transportation and planning. It wasn't easy, given the involvement of all the various bodies in Cuba sending people there. When volunteers completed their mission, replacements were sent to continue the work they were doing. The Cuban agency Cuba Técnica played an important

IV. DEFENDING ANGOLA'S SOVEREIGNTY   149

part in organizing all this.

Nor were all the Cuban volunteers in Luanda, of course. It's in Luanda that we prepared the conditions to receive the arriving Cubans and send them out to the provinces where they'd be serving. Transport was generally not by land, since UNITA had laid a lot of land mines. Road travel could only be done in caravan, with military support. Most travel was by air, and all that had to be planned and coordinated, including with the Soviets, who had cargo planes there. Cubans had to be transported in those planes, sometimes sitting on top of cargo all the way to the provinces.

By 1978, as everything was getting better organized, the technical assistance agency I mentioned was created—Cuba Técnica. At the time, it was under the Ministry of Foreign Relations. Now it works under the direction of the Ministry of Foreign Investment and Economic Collaboration.

Eventually, Cuba's collaboration was formalized in agreements, but initially it was all done on the fly. Angola would ask, and we would send.

WATERS: From 1985 to 1987 you were in Angola a third time, now heading the Cuban civilian mission in Cabinda, a province in the north separated geographically from the rest of Angola. What was special about that experience?

ZAYAS: Cabinda's status is the result of centuries of colonial plunder and imperialist domination. At the 1885 Congress of Berlin, the European colonial powers divided up Africa among themselves. So the Belgian monarchy could have sea access for its landlocked colony in the Congo, the imperialists signed treaties that cut a sliver through Portugal's colonial possessions. That's how the northern province of Cabinda came to be geographically separated from the rest of Angola. In exchange, Portugal was given a piece of territory in the east—an area rich in diamonds, close to the border with present-day Zambia—for its colony of Angola.

Cabinda is the center of Angola's oil production. Since liberation in the mid-1970s, the entire country has lived off export earnings from that oil. The main company operating there was Gulf Oil.

KOPPEL: In countries like Equatorial Guinea, due to the legacy of imperialist domination, very few people have the technical knowledge and education demanded by the oil companies. Management brings in trained personnel from the United States, from Europe, and from other imperialist countries, employing relatively few Equatorial Guineans. Was that also true in Cabinda?

ZAYAS: There were people from many countries working there, but very few from Cabinda itself. The majority came from other countries, from all over. There were even Cubans who lived outside Cuba working for Gulf Oil.

WATERS: Are the people of Cabinda from a different tribe than in other parts of northern Angola?

ZAYAS: Yes. A large part of Cabinda's people are from some of the same tribes as people in Congo-Brazzaville and the Democratic Republic of Congo, from whom they are separated by borders long ago drawn by the imperialist powers. They don't necessarily understand each other, however. They speak different dialects.

FLEC, the Cabinda Enclave Liberation Front, was active in that province. It was a tribe-based separatist movement supported by Zaire, and later by UNITA. The US government also supported it.

When I got to Cabinda in 1985, there was fighting between FLEC and the MPLA/FAPLA. FLEC was carrying out attacks on the provincial government in Cabinda, on the airport, for example. UNITA forces there were said to be giving support to FLEC. Sometimes you couldn't leave the provincial capital without protection of the armed forces. There was always danger of attacks.

KOPPEL: What were your responsibilities in Cabinda?

ZAYAS: I was head of the civilian mission overseeing all the internationalist collaborators in Cabinda from the different bodies, in health, education, communications, and so on.

Cuba's civilian collaborators in Angola were organized in contingents, by province. One of my responsibilities, for example, was to work with the forestry contingent in Cabinda. There were about four hundred forestry workers cutting timber in the Mayombe jungle there. The lumber was for export wherever the Angolans wanted to sell it, but most was bought by Cuba.

There was no way to transport the lumber by sea, however, since Cabinda doesn't have a port and is separated from the rest of Angola. The nearest port was Pointe-Noire in Congo-Brazzaville.

A tax had to be paid to the Congo government, and there was never money to pay it. So most of the lumber wasn't exported. A lot of very good timber was lost.

WATERS: How many Cubans were in Cabinda at that time?

ZAYAS: There were about six hundred Cubans on civilian missions, including the forestry contingent, doctors, teachers, and others.

We had Cuban advisers working in every government body. Cuba's Ministry of Public Health had people there to provide medical care. It was very difficult, since there wasn't enough medicine, but the Cuban doctors did wonders. There were Russian doctors too. Different specialties were covered by either Russians or Cubans. If there was a Russian orthopedist, for instance, there wouldn't be a Cuban one, unless there was a need for both.

The medicine that was needed didn't always come, so we had to ration it. Supplies for the population were sent mostly by plane, from Luanda. Some things were sent by *patana* [small boat]. Since there was no port, they came ashore on the beaches.

One thing I was asked to do—using my experience in party and government work in Las Tunas and elsewhere—was to come up with a master plan for Cabinda. A plan for agricultural production, industry, urban development, everything. That's what I was working on, and I sent for experienced planning personnel from Cuba. We ran into lots of problems due to Cabinda's level of development.

First, they didn't have the resources. I'm talking about resources of all types, human as well as material. They lacked a trained workforce. You can't put up a building using unskilled construction workers. There has to be an architect. You have to have skilled bricklayers.

I'm giving the example of constructing a building, but it's the same with any project. To build a road, it's necessary to have a plan, the right personnel, and the funding to carry it out. Without state support and planning, it can't be done. Since Cabinda has no port, to give another example, everything had to be brought in by plane, or through Pointe-Noire in Congo-Brazzaville. In all these cases, the resources were lacking.

Another problem was the view in Cabinda that it's better to import than produce. Some would even argue it's better to import chickens than to raise them, for instance. And in a certain sense, they were right. The Portuguese had chicken farms there, with incubators and all the supplies needed to raise chickens.

But when any of these things were in short supply, the poultry would die; everything would be lost. So they'd say it's better to import chickens, eggs, all of it.

WATERS: Import from where?

ZAYAS: They imported chicken, eggs, and meat from the Netherlands and elsewhere, for example. They bought products from France and other countries. They'd bring things in from Pointe-Noire in Congo-Brazzaville.

In fact, people in Cabinda largely survived through barter across the borders with Congo-Brazzaville and the Congo. They exchanged malanga—which is a tuber they grew—for clothing, for manufactured articles, and for other food. People mainly fed themselves off what they grew. They cultivated small parcels of land, minifundia. While there are vast tracts of land in Cabinda, there are no big farms or ranches. Cattle graze in the wild. There's little agricultural development.

Those who cultivate the very small plots are mostly women. It's considered women's work. Often you'd see a woman carrying two loads on her back, a bundle of firewood for cooking, plus a child.

KOPPEL: How do you size up your mission in Cabinda?

ZAYAS: Even with all the limitations, what we accomplished was positive. My mission was to try to help develop Cabinda in terms of productivity, as well as to make sure that what the Cubans did there was done right, starting with the humblest Cuban collaborator wherever he was—like doctors at the side of their patients, for example.

Many things had to be done, so Cubans there understood the role each of them had to play. And we achieved that during the two years I was in Cabinda, in addition to helping in every way possible the party and government there.

We didn't accomplish everything we wanted to do, but we fulfilled our mission. And we were grateful, since every day one learns more. Every day one gets a better understanding of the world.

WATERS: Among the hundreds of thousands of Cuban internationalists who served in Angola were Gerardo Hernández,

Fernando González, and René González. Together with Antonio Guerrero and Ramón Labañino, they are today known around the world as the Cuban Five—Cuban revolutionaries who were arrested and framed by the US government and have been doing hard-time in US prisons since 1998.[11] They are being held hostage to the refusal of the Cuban people to surrender to Washington's fifty year-old demand to return to the imperialist-dominated fold.

René served in a tank battalion in Cabinda in 1977–78. It was an experience that he said "taught me that the most beautiful things are accomplished by human beings who are imperfect, each of us giving history a little shove."

Fernando was stationed in southern Angola in the decisive years 1987–89, when Cuban and Angolan troops defeated the South African invaders at the battle of Cuito Cuanavale. He was assigned to the Information Section of the Southern

11. Known as the Cuban Five, these revolutionaries were arrested and framed up in the United States in September 1998, when the FBI announced to much fanfare that it had discovered a "Cuban spy network" in Florida. After twenty-six months in federal detention, seventeen of them in solitary confinement, the five were put on trial. In June 2001 each of them was convicted on charges of "conspiracy to act as an unregistered foreign agent." Hernández, Guerrero, and Labañino were also convicted of "conspiracy to commit espionage," and Hernández of "conspiracy to commit murder." The five were given sentences ranging from fifteen years to double life plus fifteen years. The US government has denied Adriana Pérez and Olga Salanueva, the wives of Gerardo Hernández and René González, visas to enter the US to visit their husbands.

The five had accepted assignments to monitor counterrevolutionary groups in the United States planning attacks in Cuba, and keep the Cuban government informed. Their case has generated a broad and growing international campaign to denounce the draconian sentences and harsh conditions of their imprisonment and to demand their release.

IV. DEFENDING ANGOLA'S SOVEREIGNTY

> Those who once enslaved man and sent him to the Americas perhaps never imagined that one of those peoples who received the slaves would one day send their fighters to struggle for freedom in Africa.
>
> FIDEL CASTRO
> APRIL 19, 1976*

Troops Group, processing the intelligence reports coming in from the front lines.

Gerardo led a reconnaissance platoon in Cabinda in 1989–90. "Angola was a school" for all the Cuban internationalists, including himself, he wrote in a letter from prison.

Aren't the three of them representative of the hundreds of thousands of Cubans who took part in that historic internationalist mission?

ZAYAS: The courage and integrity shown by the Five is an example to millions around the world. It's a manifestation of the same internationalism the Cuban people—including Fernando, Gerardo, and René—demonstrated in Angola. They are an example of the type of men and women produced by Cuba's socialist revolution.

The five of them were trying to stop the United States from using US-based Cuban terrorists to carry out bombings and other actions against the Cuban people. They put themselves at risk in order to defend the revolution. They've served more than twelve years in prison, but they haven't been beaten down. They know that what they did was just, that they should not be in prison. They continue to express their convictions and fight for their freedom. That is why they are considered heroes here in Cuba, and justly so.

* Fidel Castro, "Angola: African Girón," p. 110.

Angola is a brilliant, clean, honorable, transparent page in the history of the solidarity among peoples, in the history of internationalism, in the history of Cuba's contribution to the cause of freedom and advancement. Because of all of that, Angola is also a landmark in Cuban history itself. . . .

If there's anything unique about the Cuban presence in Angola—which was the continuation of our best national traditions—it was the people's massive support for it, greater than given to any similar efforts. An entire people was ready to take part in the epic struggle. Even more far-reaching and significant was the absolutely voluntary nature of the people's participation. Ours was not just a professional army, even if we take great pride in our troops' conduct in combat, in their technical preparedness—but an army of the masses, a revolutionary army of the people. . . .

As part of that unforgettable experience, giving the best of themselves, they became at the same time better patriots, firmer revolutionaries, and more committed party members while functioning as tank crew members, infantrymen, artillerymen, fortification battalion members and sappers, aircraft pilots, special troops, scouts, communications troops, rear guard service personnel, antiaircraft defense troops, motorcade forces, engineers, technicians, political workers, military counterintelligence staff members, and other Revolutionary Armed Forces and Ministry of the Interior specialists who, along with the outstanding and exemplary workers of Cubana Airlines and the merchant marine, would make the operation a success. . . .

IV. DEFENDING ANGOLA'S SOVEREIGNTY

> Faced with new and unexpected challenges, we will always be able to remember the epic of Angola with gratitude, because without Angola we would not be as strong as we are today.
>
> RAÚL CASTRO
> MAY 27, 1991[*]

Because of their conduct behind prison walls, more and more people in the world know that what is being done to them is criminal. They have carried their struggle to the world, and the US government is paying a political price for their continued imprisonment.

They're showing what the Cuban Revolution is. And they *will* return, of that we can be sure.

WATERS: The experience of Angola—to have stayed with this internationalist commitment for almost sixteen years—had a broad impact on the political consciousness of the Cuban people. Fidel once said the revolutionary spirit of voluntary labor—something both he and Che had championed during the opening years of the revolution, but had sharply declined in the 1970s and early 1980s—sought refuge during that period in defense, in the mobilization of the Territorial Troop Militia, in the work of the internationalist missions. The rectification process of the late 1980s, which included the revival of voluntary work brigades to build homes, schools, child care centers, and clinics, and then the class solidarity that enabled Cuban working people to confront and surmount the political and economic challenges to the revolution in the wake of the implosion

---

[*] Raúl Castro, Speech at ceremony welcoming last group of internationalists to return from Angola. An English translation is available online at http://lanic.utexas.edu/project/castro/db/1991/19910527.html.

of the Soviet Union—all that would have been impossible without the internationalism, without the experience of Angola.

ZAYAS: We often talk about how we've provided help to other peoples on these missions. We go to help, to teach, to collaborate.

But Cubans have also learned a great deal. Like the way doctors in Cuba are now being trained—at the side of the patient. A doctor who trains at the patient's side is really trained. It's different from the training one gets in a classroom with a video. It used to be said here that doctors really start to understand what medicine is only when they finish their studies and begin to have patients. Today we take the student to the patient beginning in their first or second year. That's a completely different kind of training. And it's a product, in part, of what we learned from our internationalist missions.

Those serving on internationalist missions have received something else. Today's generation didn't live in the Cuba of old. They see photographs of what Cuba was like then, but they don't know how life was under capitalism. It's not that there are no problems in Cuba today. But when young Cubans go on internationalist missions, they see the reality in these places firsthand, and that gives them a clearer understanding of what the revolution changed in Cuba.

Look at what's happening in Venezuela now. Don't think that the Cubans serving in Venezuela today are just helping the Venezuelans. They're also learning what life is like in a country that hasn't had five decades of socialist revolution, with a leadership like Cuba has had, which has educated the Cuban people.

Then there's the help we've given to countries facing big catastrophes—hurricanes, floods, earthquakes. Cuban doctors have gone places where people have never seen a doctor, where they may have just enough food to survive but die from lack of basic medical attention. For everyone who has gone on these missions, that kind of experience is extremely important. It creates a consciousness different from what they had before.

They go places where even news doesn't arrive, because there are no means of communication, neither radio nor television. Simple survival is the aim. Living that reality helps mould our consciousness.

Cuban volunteers on internationalist missions in other countries are learning what Cuba used to be like. They're living in the world where such conditions still exist. They're learning about capitalism, about the exploitation of man by man.

So it's not only about helping. We also receive.

THE COVER PHOTO

Capturing a Moment
in Revolutionary History

Capturing a Moment in Revolutionary History: The Cover Photo

MARY-ALICE WATERS

The photograph on the cover of this book captures a high point in the history of the men and women who made the Cuban Revolution. Taken by Raúl Corrales, one of the revolution's great photographers, the picture shows a militia unit of workers and farmers riding to the headquarters of the United Fruit Company near the town of Mayarí in eastern Cuba on May 14, 1960, to inform its management that the company's massive holdings had been expropriated, that these lands and buildings had become the property of Cuba.

In April 1960, a year after the first of the revolution's two deepgoing agrarian reform laws began to be carried out, a group of sugar cane farmers and agricultural laborers working one of the vast plantations of the United Fruit Company and nearby farms wrote a letter to the National Institute of Agrarian Reform (INRA). They asked the revolutionary government to do something about United Fruit's refusal to share the water it piped to its domains with workers and farmers who lived on or near their property.

A few weeks later, an INRA delegation visited United Fruit's offices at the company's Preston sugar mill in what is today Holguín province. They presented the farmers' and workers' request for access to water. According to an account by INRA's executive director at the time, Antonio Núñez Jiménez, the company's answer "was an insolent 'No.'"[1]

The next day, in response, Prime Minister Fidel Castro signed an order expropriating the more than 270,000 acres, nearly 425 square miles of Cuban land, held by United Fruit— a name that had become so hated throughout Latin America that the company later decided to reinvent itself as Chiquita Brands International. The wealthy US capitalist families who own the corporation had extensive landholdings throughout Central America and the Caribbean, including in Nicaragua, Guatemala, Costa Rica, and Panama, whose rulers had so often been subordinated to imperialist interests through a combination of bribery and, when necessary, naked force.

The expropriation decree included the Preston sugar mill and all US-owned property on the plantation. United Fruit was to receive compensation of 6,150,207 Cuban pesos[2] in twenty-year Agrarian Reform bonds paying an annual interest of 4.5 percent. The same terms were given other big landowners expropriated under the 1959 agrarian reform law. That law set a limit of roughly 1,000 acres on individual landholdings, transferred property in excess of that limit to the new government, and granted sharecroppers, tenant farmers, and squatters title to the land they tilled.

Interest on the agrarian reform bonds was to be paid from the sugar "quota," the amount of Cuban sugar guaranteed for sale each year in the United States. Compensation was based on the assessed value of the holdings of United Fruit and other big landowners, which in turn was based on the value

1. Antonio Núñez Jiménez, *En Marcha con Fidel: 1960* [On the march with Fidel: 1960] (Havana: Antonio Núñez Jiménez Foundation for Nature and Man, 1998), pp. 122–26.

2. A peso was roughly equivalent to one US dollar at the time.

the companies themselves had declared for tax purposes a year and a half earlier, in October 1958.

In face of outraged cries from Washington and other imperialist governments and their mouthpieces—"Confiscation!" screamed the headline in *Time* magazine's June 1, 1959, issue—Fidel Castro explained the necessity of the revolutionary government's land reform in his address to the United Nations General Assembly in September 1960.[3]

"In our country [the land reform] was indispensable," the Cuban leader told the delegates, speaking over the UN's marble rostrum to revolutionary-minded working people and youth around the world. "More than 200,000 peasant families lived in the countryside without land with which to plant essential foodstuffs. Without agrarian reform our country could not have taken the first step toward development," he said—toward solving "the great unemployment problem on the land" and "the frightful poverty that existed in the rural areas of our country."

As to the compensation paid to the expropriated capitalist families, Castro said, "Notes from the U.S. State Department began to rain down on Cuba. They never asked us about our problems [or] their responsibility in creating the problems. They never asked us how many died of starvation in our country, how many were suffering from tuberculosis, how many were unemployed." Instead, he said, the State Department "demanded three things: 'prompt, adequate, and effective compensation.' Do you understand that language?" Castro asked. "That means, 'Pay this instant, in

3. "The Case of Cuba Is the Case of All Underdeveloped Countries: Address to General Assembly, September 26, 1960," in Fidel Castro and Che Guevara, *To Speak the Truth: Why Washington's 'Cold War' against Cuba Doesn't End* (Pathfinder, 1992). The excerpts cited here are from pages 47–48 [2010 printing].

dollars, and whatever we ask.'"

The arrogant response of the owners of United Fruit to the Cuban government's compensation offer was no different. While the giant corporation had "acquired" its vast landholdings for well under a penny an acre (some $817 all told!)—at the turn of the twentieth century, when the island was under direct US military occupation—its owners demanded that the Cuban government pay them more than $56 million for the expropriated land.

A few months later, in retaliation against the expropriation of US-owned properties and other measures taken by the revolutionary government in the interests of Cuba's working people, the US rulers ended all sugar imports from Cuba. With that unilateral act, Washington rendered null and void redemption of the bonds. The US government's abolition of the quota was soon followed by a full-fledged economic embargo of Cuba that remains in effect to this day.

The mounted militia squad on the cover is reminiscent of the nineteenth-century *mambi* army units, often composed primarily of combatants who had been slaves or bonded Chinese laborers. After thirty years of revolutionary struggle, that army won Cuba's independence from Spain in 1898. The pictured *mambises* of May 14, 1960, included many of the farmers who had written to INRA only a few weeks before.

The ceremony where the expropriation was officially proclaimed was held on the golf course that had been reserved for United Fruit Company bosses and their friends. Those assembled learned that the new name of the mill was to be "Guatemala"—in honor of the people of that country, whose government had been overthrown in 1954 in a US-organized coup to reverse a land reform affecting holdings of United Fruit and other US corporations there.

Among the first measures implemented by INRA in the

area was to give the toilers the authorization and means to install pipes to provide water from the former United Fruit's aqueduct to neighboring farmers.

The new administration of the Guatemala mill, with the armed support of the revolutionary government, also put an end to segregated living quarters on the United Fruit plantation, where, Nuñez noted, there were "neighborhoods with borders, so that blacks and whites, Americans and Cubans, could not live together or intermingle." There was even a neighborhood called Brooklyn "where the poorest and blackest live," while "near the bay, in brand-new buildings with luxurious gardens, are the homes of the Americans and their Cuban lackeys...."

Prior to 1944, Nuñez recalled to those celebrating United Fruit's expropriation, the company had refused to allow a public school on the grounds of the sugar mill, or the construction of additional roads to connect the plantation with the Central Highway. "They wanted to keep this region isolated, closed off to all progress, to have us isolated here as if it were—and it was, in fact—a separate republic."

■

In late 2010, as the final editing of *Soldier of the Cuban Revolution* by Alfonso Zayas was under way, an exhibit entitled "Cuba in Revolution" opened at New York City's International Center of Photography. It was widely acclaimed in newspapers and magazines across the country. Of the more than 180 evocative photos on display at the museum—from prerevolutionary Cuba of the early 1950s, through 1968—the photograph by Raúl Corrales that serves as the cover of this book was selected by the curators as the image used on press releases and brochures for the show. It was reproduced as part of reviews of the exhibit in newspapers as varied as the *New York Times*, the *Militant*, and the *Boston Globe*, and magazines such as *Art Daily* and *Art Info*.

As the exhibit brought home to those of us fortunate enough to see it, the photographic record of the Cuban Revolution draws its power from the joy and creativity, the youth, humor, and enthusiasm of Cuba's working people. That love of life and determination to struggle was captured on film as they set about laying the foundations of a new social order and defending their newly conquered freedom with discipline and arms, with their lives.

From that same wellspring, world-famous Cuban photojournalists of the epoch, including Alberto Korda, Osvaldo Salas, Liborio Noval, and Corrales himself, developed their craft and created a priceless legacy. That some of their photos have enriched the covers and internal pages of books published by Pathfinder Press over the last two decades, and in that way can be shared more widely with revolutionary-minded working people around the world, is a source of great satisfaction.

December 2010

Glossary of Individuals, Organizations, and Events

Acevedo, Rogelio (1941–) – Joined Rebel Army July 1957; national director of revolutionary militias 1960. Second in command of military mission in Angola 1975–76. Division general of Revolutionary Armed Forces.

Acosta, Armando (1920–2009) – Member of Popular Socialist Party who joined Column 8 led by Che Guevara and participated in westward invasion. Became commander in Rebel Army. General secretary of Communist Party in Oriente province until 1966. Later national coordinator of Committees for the Defense of the Revolution. Member of Communist Party Central Committee 1965–91.

Alayón, Pelayo (d. 1959) – Captain in Batista army. Tried by revolutionary tribunal for war atrocities, convicted, and executed.

Almeida, Juan (1927–2009) – Recruited to revolutionary movement led by Fidel Castro and participant in 1953 Moncada attack. Sentenced to ten years in prison; released with other Moncada prisoners May 1955 following national amnesty campaign. Participated in *Granma* expedition 1956. Promoted to commander Feb. 1958; headed Third Eastern Front. After 1959 responsibilities included head of air force, vice minister of Revolutionary Armed Forces, and vice president of Council of State. One of three Sierra combatants with rank of

Commander of the Revolution. Member of Communist Party Central Committee and Political Bureau from its founding in 1965. Hero of the Republic of Cuba. President of Association of Combatants of the Cuban Revolution at time of death.

Álvarez, Miguel – Combatant in Column 8 commanded by Che Guevara during march from Oriente to Las Villas province. Platoon commander at command post in Escambray. Rank of captain at end of war. Member of FAR, retired with rank of colonel.

Alves, Nito (1945–1977) – MPLA leader in Angola's fight against Portuguese colonialism; named interior minister at independence Nov. 1975. Led faction in MPLA; expelled and arrested May 1977. His supporters carried out attempted coup against government of Agostinho Neto. Executed after coup's defeat.

Ameijeiras, Efigenio (1931–) – *Granma* expeditionary in 1956. Finished war as commander of Column 6 and second in command of Second Eastern Front. As head of Revolutionary National Police, led its battalion at Bay of Pigs 1961. Commanded Cuban internationalist contingent in Algeria 1963. In 1984 served as a leader of Cuba's military mission in Angola. Division general in FAR.

Association of Combatants of the Cuban Revolution (ACRC) – Founded 1993 as organization of fighters from Rebel Army, urban clandestine struggle, Playa Girón, struggle against counterrevolutionary bands, and Cuba's internationalist missions, both military and civilian. Composed of more than 300,000 members who work to transmit revolution's history and lessons to new generations.

Authentic Organization – Military organization set up by leaders of Authentic Party to oppose Batista following 1952 coup.

Authentic Party (Cuban Revolutionary Party) – Bourgeois-nationalist party formed 1934, popularly known as *auténticos*, claiming to be authentic followers of José Martí's Cuban Revolutionary Party. In power 1944–52 under presidents Ramón Grau and Carlos Prío. Part of bourgeois opposition to Batista 1952–58. As revolution deepened 1959–60, main *auténtico* leaders left Cuba for US and joined counterrevolutionary forces.

Batista, Fulgencio (1901–1973) – Military strongman in Cuba 1934–44. Led coup on March 10, 1952, establishing military-police tyranny. Fled Cuba Jan. 1, 1959, in face of advancing Rebel Army and popular insurrection.

Bermúdez, Alcibíades (d. 1964) – Member of July 26 Movement in Puerto Padre. Rebel Army officer during revolutionary war. After victory of revolution successfully infiltrated counterrevolutionary bands. Died in accident.

Bordón, Víctor (1930–) – Member of July 26 Movement in Las Villas; formed guerrilla unit there late 1956. In Oct. 1958 unit was integrated into front led by Che Guevara. Attained rank of commander. Subsequently held national leadership responsibilities in Ministry of Construction in Matanzas. Director of Cometal Enterprise Group.

Caetano, Jacobo (Monstruo Inmortal) – Popular Movement for the Liberation of Angola (MPLA) member; political commissar in Angolan army. Supporter of 1977 attempted coup. Captured and executed.

Camacho, Julio (1924–) – A founder of July 26 Movement in Guantánamo 1955; its coordinator and action chief there. A leader of Nov. 30, 1956, uprising in that city. Helped lead Sept. 5, 1957, uprising in Cienfuegos; subsequently joined Rebel Army. Member of Communist Party Central Committee since its founding in 1965. Responsibilities have included minister of transportation; leadership positions in FAR; first secretary of CP provincial committees in Pinar del Río, City of Havana, and Santiago de Cuba; ambassador to Soviet Union.

Carreira, Iko (1933–2000) – Officer in Portuguese army; deserted to join MPLA in Angola's war for independence. Angola's minister of defense and army commander-in-chief 1975–85.

Casillas, Joaquín (1907–1959) – Cuban army officer. In 1948 murdered sugar workers leader Jesús Menéndez in Manzanillo during sugar workers strike, but was acquitted. Following Batista's 1952 coup, promoted to major and then lt. colonel. Head of military regiment in Santa Clara during revolutionary war; captured after city fell to Rebel Army, Jan. 1, 1959. Killed trying to escape.

Castellanos, Alberto (1934–) – Rebel Army combatant in Che Guevara's column; part of Guevara's escort in 1959. Volunteered for 1963–64 mission in Argentina to support guerrilla unit led by Jorge Ricardo Masetti. Captured Feb. 1964; imprisoned in Argentina until 1967, never revealing identity as a Cuban. Returned to Cuba after release.

Castro, Fidel (1926–) – Organized and led revolutionary movement against Batista tyranny that carried out July 26, 1953, attack on Moncada garrison in Santiago de Cuba and Carlos Manuel de Céspedes garrison in Bayamo. Captured, tried, and sentenced to fifteen years in prison. Released 1955 after national amnesty campaign. Led founding of July 26 Revolutionary Movement. Organized *Granma* expedition from Mexico to launch revolutionary war in Cuba, late 1956. Commander of Rebel Army from founding. Following triumph was Cuba's prime minister Feb. 1959 to 1976. President of Council of State and Council of Ministers 1976–2008; commander in chief of Revolutionary Armed Forces (1959–2008). From its founding in 1965, first secretary of Communist Party of Cuba.

Castro, Raúl (1931–) – An organizer of student protests at University of Havana against Batista dictatorship. Participated in 1953 Moncada attack. Captured and sentenced to thirteen years in prison. Released May 1955 following national amnesty campaign. Founding member of July 26 Movement and participant in 1956 *Granma* expedition. Promoted to commander in Rebel Army, Feb. 1958; headed Second Eastern Front. Minister of Revolutionary Armed Forces 1959–2008. Vice premier from 1959 until 1976. First vice president of Council of State and Council of Ministers 1976–2008; acting president since 2006; president since 2008. Since 1965 second secretary of Communist Party of Cuba.

Castro Mercader, Raúl (1937–) – Member of July 26 Movement from Puerto Padre. One of three who attacked the explosives depot there in 1956. Joined Rebel Army March 1957 as part of first group of reinforcements (Marabuzaleros). In August 1957 promoted to captain in Column 4 led by Che Guevara. Served in Angola as internationalist combatant. Brigadier general in Revolutionary Armed Forces; retired from active duty.

Chomón, Faure (1929–) – Leader of Revolutionary Directorate and survivor of March 13, 1957, attack on Presidential Palace. Organized Feb. 1958 expedition establishing guerrilla front in Escambray mountains. Part of Las Villas front commanded by Che Guevara after Oct. 1958. Member Communist Party Central Committee since 1965; has served as Cuba's ambassador to Soviet Union, Vietnam, and Ecuador. Deputy in National Assembly of People's Power since 1976.

Cienfuegos, Camilo (1932–1959) – *Granma* expeditionary 1956. Captain in Rebel Army Column 4 led by Che Guevara, promoted to commander in August 1958. From Aug. to Oct. 1958 led Column 2 westward from Sierra Maestra en route to Pinar del Río. Operated in northern Las Villas until end of war. Became Rebel Army chief of staff, Jan. 1959. Killed when plane lost at sea while returning to Havana, Oct. 28, 1959.

Colomé, Abelardo (1939–) – Joined Rebel Army March 1957, reaching rank of commander. Served in Argentina and Bolivia 1962–64 to prepare and support guerrilla front in Argentina led by Jorge Ricardo Masetti. Headed Cuban mission in Angola 1975–76. Member Communist Party Central Committee and Political Bureau, and a vice president of Cuba's Council of State. Interior minister since 1989. Holds rank of army corps general.

Colono – In prerevolutionary Cuba, the term *colono* was used to refer to sugarcane farmers, among whom there were class differences. In eastern Cuba many were tenant farmers who rented land from the owners of mills. Others held title to their land, even if they were heavily indebted, and were contracted to sell their cane exclusively to one mill. Some farm families relied on their own labor, while others hired workers to help harvest the cane. A handful were well-off enough to aspire to becoming big landowners themselves. Colonos were overwhelmingly of European background, principally from Spain. Rural toilers who were Black were mostly agricultural workers (freed slaves had been denied the right to own or rent land). The colono system transferred to individual small farmers the economic risk of growing sugar as well as the responsibility for hiring and firing seasonal labor.

Committees for the Defense of the Revolution (CDRs) – Organized in 1960 on block-by-block basis as a tool through which Cuban people could exercise vigilance against counterrevolutionary activity. In subsequent years have also served as a vehicle to organize participation in vaccination and other public health campaigns, civil defense, the fight against petty crime, and other civic tasks.

Crespo, Luis (1923–2002) – Participant in Granma expedition; served in Rebel Army Column 1. Ended war with rank of commander.

CTC – Founded in 1939 as the Confederation of Cuban Workers, with members of Popular Socialist party in major leadership positions until 1947, when driven out during Cold War anticommunist witch hunt. Officialdom supported Batista dictatorship after 1952. Reorganized after 1959 as CTC-Revolutionary. In 1961 changed name to Central Organization of Cuban Workers, retaining original initials.

de la Fe, Ernesto (1913–1992) – Journalist for daily Prensa Libre, named minister of information after Batista's 1952 coup. Arrested Jan. 1959, tried and sentenced to 15 years in prison; later went to United States.

Díaz, Epifanio (d. 1964) – Peasant in Sierra Maestra who provided aid to Rebel Army.

Domínguez, Guillermo (1932–1957) – Member of July 26 Movement urban underground in Puerto Padre; joined Rebel Army March 1957 as part of first group of reinforcements (Marabuzaleros), becoming lieutenant. Captured and killed May 17, 1957.

Espín, Vilma (1930–2007) – Founding member of July 26 Movement in Santiago de Cuba. Close collaborator of Frank País, helped organize Nov. 30, 1956, uprising in Santiago; later July 26 Movement coordinator in Oriente province. Joined Rebel Army July 1958, serving in Second Eastern Front. President Federation of Cuban Women from 1960 until death. Member of Communist Party Central Committee from 1965 and Political Bureau 1980–91. Member of Council of State from 1976.

Evaristo, Eduardo (Bakaloff) – Angolan army chief of staff. Member of Political Bureau of MPLA; FAPLA chief of operations. Supporter of 1977 attempted coup. Captured and executed.

FAPLA (People's Armed Forces for the Liberation of Angola) – Originating as armed wing of MPLA in fight against Portuguese colonialism, became Angola's armed forces following independence in 1975.

FAR *See* Revolutionary Armed Forces.

Federation of Cuban Women (FMC) – Founded August 23, 1960, with Vilma Espín as president. United prorevolution women's organizations. Championing fight for women's equality, has worked to integrate women into revolution's tasks and labor force.

Fernández, José Ramón (1923–) – A first lieutenant in Cuban army, he opposed Batista dictatorship and helped organize "Los Puros" conspiracy of officers opposed to regime. Court-martialed 1956 and sentenced to six years in prison on Isle of Pines, where he established political relations with July 26 Movement. Incorporated in Rebel Army 1959; served as director of Militia Leadership School. Led main column that repelled Bay of Pigs invasion April 1961. Deputy minister of FAR until 1970; minister of education 1972–91. Vice president of Council of Ministers since 1978.

Fernández Mell, Oscar (1931–) – Captain in Che Guevara's Rebel Army column; promoted to commander after 1959 triumph. A physician, he served in various posts, including chief of staff of Western Army, deputy chief of staff of Ministry of the Revolutionary Armed Forces, and Cuba's ambassador to Britain.

Fernández Monte de Oca, Alberto (1935–1967) – Member of July 26 Movement urban underground in Santiago de Cuba and then Santa Clara. Joined Rebel Army Nov. 1958, serving with Column 8. Held rank of captain in armed forces. Combatant in guerrilla movement in Bolivia with Che Guevara 1966–67 under nom de guerre *Pacho*; killed in battle.

FLEC (Front for the Liberation of the Enclave of Cabinda) – Formed 1963 to fight Portuguese colonialism in Cabinda. Following Angola's independence in 1975 FLEC forces fought against MPLA-led Angolan government, advocating independence for Cabinda.

FNLA (National Front for the Liberation of Angola) – Formed 1962 and led by Holden Roberto. One of armed groups in struggle against Portuguese colonialism; developed ties with CIA and dictatorship in Zaire. Backed by Zaire and South

Africa, waged war against Angolan government following independence in 1975.

Frías, Ciro (1928–1958) – Peasant from Sierra Maestra; joined Rebel Army Jan. 1957 and became a captain. Member of Column 18 of Second Eastern Front led by Raúl Castro. Killed in battle April 10, 1958; posthumously promoted to commander.

García, Armando (1927–1957) – Member of July 26 Movement national leadership from Santiago. Captured, tortured, and murdered by Batista police.

García, Calixto (1931–) – Participated in July 26, 1953, attack on Bayamo garrison; escaped and went to Costa Rica where, in Nov. 1953, he was the first member of the July 26 Movement Che Guevara met. A *Granma* expeditionary, he finished revolutionary war as commander in Third Front. After 1959 headed Eastern and Central Armies and held other military posts in FAR and Communist Party. A member of CP Central Committee 1965–80. Currently a brigadier general.

García, Guillermo (1928–) – Peasant from Sierra Maestra who became member of July 26 Movement cell. From early 1957, combatant in Column 1 led by Fidel Castro. Promoted to commander in Third Eastern Front led by Juan Almeida, late 1958. Member Communist Party Central Committee since 1965, Political Bureau 1965–86. Minister of transportation 1974–85. Member of Council of State. One of three Sierra combatants to hold title Commander of the Revolution.

García, Rigoberto (1932–) – Joined Rebel Army Feb. 1957, serving in Fidel Castro's column, then under Juan Almeida. Member of Communist Party Central Committee since 1975; head of Youth Army of Labor (EJT) 1979–2007. Army corps general.

Gómez, Máximo (1836–1905) – Born in Dominican Republic, fought in independence war in Cuba 1868–78. Major general of Liberation Army by end of conflict. When war relaunched in 1895, returned to Cuba as general-in-chief of Cuban independence army.

Gómez Ochoa, Delio (1929–) – Rebel Army fighter. After failure of April 1958 general strike attempt, became national action coordinator of July 26 Movement based in Havana. Became commander of Rebel Column 32 and of Fourth Eastern Front October 1958. After revolution's victory, led armed expedition to Dominican Republic June 1959 by Dominican and Cuban volunteers; captured and later released. Subsequently had responsibilities in agricultural sector in Cuba.

Grau, Ricardo José (d. 1959) – Colonel in Batista army. Tried by revolutionary tribunal for war atrocities, convicted, and executed.

Grau San Martín, Ramón (1889–1969) – Founding leader of Cuban Revolutionary (Authentic) Party 1934. Cuba's president 1944–48. During Batista dictatorship of 1952–58, advocated "electoral solution" and opposed July 26 Movement's course. Retired from political activity, he remained in Cuba until his death.

Guerra Matos, Felipe (Guerrita) (1927–) – Leader of July 26 Movement in Manzanillo. Rebel Army captain. Named head of National Institute of Sports 1959.

Guevara, Ernesto Che (1928–1967) – Argentine-born leader of Cuban Revolution. Recruited in Mexico in 1955 to *Granma* expedition as troop doctor. First Rebel Army combatant promoted to commander, 1957. After 1959 held responsibilities including head of National Bank and minister of industry. Led Cuban column fighting alongside anti-imperialist forces in Congo 1965. Led guerrilla detachment in Bolivia 1966–67. Wounded and captured during CIA-organized counterguerrilla operation, Oct. 8, 1967. Murdered following day. In October 1997 the remains of Guevara and others who died fighting in Bolivia were returned to Cuba.

Guiteras, Antonio (1906–1935) – Student leader of fight against Gerardo Machado dictatorship in 1920s and '30s. Leader of anti-imperialist forces during 1933 revolutionary upsurge that overthrew Machado; interior minister in Hundred Days Government overthrown in Batista coup Jan. 1934. Founder of revolutionary organization Young Cuba. Killed May 8, 1935, while leading clandestine struggle against first Batista regime.

Gutiérrez Menoyo, Eloy (1934–) – Leader of Second National Front of the Escambray, which was expelled from Revolutionary Directorate in 1958 for extortion and abuse of peasants and close ties to bourgeois forces in anti-Batista opposition. Left Cuba 1960; returned with counterrevolutionary armed band Dec. 1964. Captured and imprisoned until 1986. Formed Miami-based Cambio Cubano (Cuban Change). Returned to Cuba 2003 to be part of a "loyal opposition."

Hart, Armando (1930–) – A leader of Revolutionary National Movement following Batista's 1952 coup. In 1955 was founding member of July 26 Movement and a leader of its urban underground. Its national coordinator from early 1957 to Jan. 1958, when captured and imprisoned until Jan. 1, 1959. Minister of education 1959–65; Communist Party organization secretary 1965–70; minister of culture 1976–97. Member of Communist Party Central Committee since 1965, serving on Political Bureau 1965–86.

Hernández, Hernando (1910–1968) – Brigadier general and head of National Police under Batista 1956–57. Arrested Jan. 1959; sentenced to prison by revolutionary tribunal.

Iglesias, Joel (1941–) – From peasant family, joined Rebel Army 1957, serving under Che Guevara; promoted to commander at end of war. First president of Association of Rebel Youth 1960, becoming general secretary of Union of Young Communists 1962. Member of CP Central Committee 1965–75.

July 26 Revolutionary Movement – Founded June 1955 by Fidel Castro and other participants in Moncada attack, together with other revolutionary forces. During war against tyranny was composed of Rebel Army in mountains (*Sierra*) and underground network in cities and countryside (*Llano*— "plains"). In May 1958 national leadership was centralized in Sierra Maestra; Fidel Castro was chosen general secretary. Led fusion with Popular Socialist Party and Revolutionary Directorate in 1961.

Lara, Lúcio (1929–) – Founding member of MPLA and longtime member of its Central Committee. MPLA organization secretary during Angolan civil war.

Lobo, Julio (1898–1983) – Known as the "King of Sugar," prior to the revolution Lobo was the richest man in Cuba. Through trading offices around the world he controlled half of sugar sales to the US from Cuba, Puerto Rico, and the Philippines. Owned fourteen mills in Cuba and more than 345,000 acres (some 540 square miles) of land. Left Cuba in 1960 after holdings were expropriated, rejecting offer from new revolutionary government to remain and help reorganize sugar industry. Went bankrupt trading sugar in US in 1964 and retired to Spain.

Maceo, Antonio (1845–1896) – Military leader and strategist in Cuba's 19th century wars of independence from Spain. Known in Cuba as Bronze Titan, led 1895–96 westward march from Oriente to Pinar del Río province. At conclusion of first war in 1878, became symbol of revolutionary intransigence by refusing to put down arms in an action known as Baraguá Protest. Killed in battle.

Marabuzaleros – First major group of reinforcements to join Rebel Army, March 1957. Named after the dense, thorny *marabú* thicket outside Manzanillo, where they assembled before marching up into Sierra Maestra. The 51 new recruits had taken part in support actions for *Granma* landing three months earlier. Their arrival more than tripled size of rebel forces.

Martínez Rosales, Alberto (Kiko) – Member of vanguard platoon of Ciro Redondo Column 8 commanded by Guevara that invaded western Cuba. Fought in battle of Santa Clara. Member of FAR. Retired with rank of colonel.

Matos, Huber (1918–) – Small landowner in Oriente province; joined Rebel Army March 1958, becoming commander of Column 9. As military head of Camagüey province in Oct. 1959, arrested for organizing attempted mutiny; imprisoned until 1979. Currently lives in US and heads counterrevolutionary Cuba Independent and Democratic.

Matthews, Herbert (1900–1977) – *New York Times* correspondent. On Feb. 17, 1957, was first journalist to interview and photograph Fidel Castro in Sierra Maestra, disproving Batista regime's lie that rebels had been wiped out.

Menéndez, Jesús (1911–1948) – General secretary of National Federation of Sugar Workers and leader of Popular Socialist Party. Murdered in Manzanillo by army captain Joaquín Casillas Jan. 1948.

Miret, Pedro (1927–) – A leader of 1953 Moncada attack; sentenced to 13 years in prison. Released in May 1955 amnesty; a founding leader of July 26 Movement. During revolutionary war became a Rebel Army commander. Member of Communist Party Central Committee since 1965. Member of Council of State and vice president of Council of Ministers.

Mobutu Sese Seko (1930–1997) – Army chief of staff in newly independent Congo; led coup against Patrice Lumumba Sept. 1960. Following Lumumba's murder in Jan. 1961, became country's strongman. In 1965 proclaimed himself president, holding power until overthrown in 1997. Born Joseph Mobutu, he changed his name in 1972.

Moracén, Rafael (1939–) – Joined Rebel Army 1958. Served in internationalist missions in Congo-Brazzaville 1965–67, Syria 1973, Angola 1975–82. Holds rank of brigadier general. Hero of the Republic of Cuba. Head of international relations for Association of Combatants of Cuban Revolution.

Morales, Calixto (1929–) – *Granma* expeditionary and Rebel Army combatant; was assigned to work in Santiago underground from Sept. 1957 to March 1958. Subsequently a captain in Che Guevara's column. In early 1960s worked with Guevara in Ministry of Industry.

Morejón, Pedro (d. 1959) – Colonel in Batista army. Tried by revolutionary tribunal for war atrocities, convicted, and executed.

Morgan, William (1928–1961) – Former US soldier; became a leader of Second National Front of the Escambray. Following fall of Batista, set up frog farm, used to channel supplies to US-backed counterrevolutionary bands in Escambray mountains. After joining these bands, was captured by FAR, tried, and executed.

MPLA (Popular Movement for the Liberation of Angola) – Founded 1956 to wage armed struggle for Angola's independence from Portugal. From 1962 led by Agostinho Neto. Following independence in 1975 became governing party.

National Association of Small Farmers (ANAP) – Organization of Cuban farmers founded 1961. Aids and represents farmers working individually held land and members of farming cooperatives.

Neto, Agostinho (1922–1979) – Leader of fight against Portuguese colonialism in Angola. President of MPLA from 1962; president of Angola 1975 until his death.

Núñez Jiménez, Antonio (1923–1998) – Internationally known geographer and specialist on caves. Joined Guevara's column on eve of battle of Santa Clara, with rank of captain. Responsibilities after 1959 included executive director of National Institute of Agrarian Reform, president of Academy of Sciences, vice minister of culture, ambassador to Peru.

October 1962 "Missile" Crisis – In face of Washington's preparations to invade Cuba in early 1962, Havana signed a mutual defense agreement with Moscow that included installation of Soviet nuclear missiles. In October 1962 US president John Kennedy demanded removal of missiles and ordered blockade of island by US warships. Washington placed US forces on nuclear alert and stepped up preparations to invade. Cuban workers and farmers mobilized in millions to defend the revolution. On October 28 Soviet premier Nikita Khrushchev, without consulting Cuban government, announced Moscow's decision to remove missiles.

País, Frank (1934–1957) – Vice president of Federation of University Students in Oriente. Central leader of Revolutionary National Action and later of Revolutionary National Movement (MNR). Joined in founding July 26 Movement and became its central leader in Oriente province, its national action coordinator, and head of its urban militias. Murdered by dictatorship's forces July 30, 1957.

Pena, Félix (1930–1959) – Participant in Nov. 30, 1956, Santiago de Cuba uprising. Member of first reinforcement contingent (Marabuzaleros); participated in Columns 1, 6, and 18; promoted to commander.

Pérez, Crescencio (1895–1986) – Member of July 26 Movement cell in Sierra Maestra prior to *Granma* landing. Among first peasants to join Rebel Army, finishing war as commander of Column 7. Following triumph of revolution, carried various responsibilities in FAR.

Popular Socialist Party (PSP) – Name taken by Communist Party of Cuba in 1944 when part of Batista's government. Opposed Batista dictatorship after 1952 coup but rejected revolutionary political course of July 26 Movement. Collaborated with the latter in final months of revolutionary war. Fused with July 26 Movement and Revolutionary Directorate 1961.

Prío Socarrás, Carlos (1903–1977) – Leader of Authentic Party and president of Cuba from 1948 until Batista's 1952 coup. Leading figure in bourgeois opposition during revolutionary war. In early 1961 left Cuba and went to US.

Pupo Peña, Orlando – Member of July 26 Movement in Puerto Padre; took part in attack on explosives depot 1956. Joined Rebel Army March 1957 as member of first group of reinforcements (Marabuzaleros); served in Column 1. Member of commander-in-chief's escort. Carried out international mission in Cape Verde 1990–92. Retired from FAR with rank of colonel.

Ramos Latour, René (1932–1958) – July 26 Movement national action coordinator after Frank País's death, heading its urban militias. Joined Rebel Army as a commander May 1958. Killed in battle July 30, 1958, at end of Batista army's offensive in Sierra Maestra.

Rectification process – Political policies implemented in Cuba between 1986 and early 1990s, marking turn away from economic management and planning policies used in Soviet Union and Eastern Europe, which were soon to help precipitate the collapse of bureaucratic regimes and parties in those countries. As the economic and political crisis known as the Special Period accelerated from 1990 on, and resources dwindled, many measures associated with rectification, such as the spread of volunteer work brigades to build badly needed housing, had to be shelved.

Redondo, Ciro (1931–1957) – Participated in 1953 Moncada attack; captured, tried, and sentenced to 10 years in prison. Released in May 1955 following national amnesty campaign. A *Granma* expeditionary, he became a captain in Rebel Army, serving in Guevara's column. Killed in battle Nov. 29, 1957; posthumously promoted to commander.

Revolutionary Armed Forces (FAR) – Continuator of Rebel Army, led by Fidel Castro, that waged Cuba's revolutionary war, 1956–58. FAR was established October 1959, consolidating under single command structure Rebel Army, Rebel Air Force, Revolutionary Navy, and Revolutionary National Police. Raúl Castro became head of the Ministry of the Revolutionary Armed Forces (MINFAR) at its inception, a responsibility he held until 2008.

Revolutionary Directorate – Formed in 1955 by José Antonio Echeverría and other leaders of Federation of University Students (FEU). Organized March 13, 1957, attack on Presidential Palace in which a number of its central leaders were killed, including Echeverría. In early 1958 organized guerrilla column in Escambray mountains of Las Villas, which later became part of front commanded by Che Guevara. Fused with July 26 Movement and Popular Socialist Party in 1961.

Risquet, Jorge (1930–) – Popular Socialist Party member in Rebel Army; secretary of Integrated Revolutionary Organizations (ORI) in Oriente Province after March 1962; later served as minister of labor; went to Congo-Brazzaville in 1965 to assist liberation forces; member of Communist Party Central Committee since 1965. Head of civilian mission in Angola 1975–80.

Roberto, Holden (1923–2007) – Cofounded Angola's first nationalist movement 1956. In 1962 founding leader of FNLA. Worked with CIA and dictatorship in Zaire.

Rodríguez, Roberto "Vaquerito" (1935–1958) – Rebel Army captain; headed "Suicide Squad," which took on most dangerous combat missions in Column 8 commanded by Che Guevara; killed in battle of Santa Clara, Dec. 30, 1958.

Sánchez, Celia (1920–1980) – A leader in Oriente province of amnesty campaign for imprisoned Moncadistas. Founding member of July 26 Movement in 1955 and its central organizer in Manzanillo. Organized urban supply and recruitment network for Rebel Army. First woman to become a Rebel Army combatant, serving on its general command from Oct. 1957. At her death a member of Communist Party Central Committee and secretary of Council of State and Council of Ministers.

Sánchez, Universo (1929–) – *Granma* expeditionary; became Rebel Army commander. Currently a retired officer in Cuban armed forces.

Sánchez Mosquera, Ángel (d. 2008) – Lieutenant in Batista army notorious for brutality against peasants; ended war as a colonel. Fled Cuba Jan. 1, 1959.

Savimbi, Jonas (1934–2002) – In 1960 joined movement for Angola's independence from Portugal. Founded UNITA in 1966; its central leader. In 1975 allied with South Africa and US to overthrow MPLA-led government of newly independent country. Led civil war against government for more than 25 years. Killed by Angolan government forces.

Schueg Colás, Víctor (1936–1998) – Joined Rebel Army 1958, serving under Raúl Castro. Carried out internationalist mission in Congo 1965 as part of Che Guevara's column. Served in Angola 1975–76 as chief of staff of Cuban military mission. Head of Central Army 1987–88. Brigadier general in FAR. Alternate member Communist Party Central Committee 1980–86, full member 1986–91.

Second National Front of the Escambray – Armed group in Las Villas led by Eloy Gutiérrez Menoyo. Formed Nov. 10, 1957, on initiative of Revolutionary Directorate; betrayed Directorate's political goals and terrorized peasants in Escambray, for which it was expelled from Directorate in mid-1958. Refused to collaborate with Guevara's forces and other revolutionary units. Most of its leaders joined counterrevolution after 1959.

Sosa, Merob (1920–1975) – Officer of Batista army in Sierra Maestra notorious for crimes and abuses against rural population.

Sosa Blanco, Jesús (c.1907–1959) – Major in Batista army, commanding its garrison in Holguín. Arrested January 1959 and charged with 56 murders; tried before revolutionary tribunal, convicted, and executed.

Sotto, Pedro (1935–1958) – *Granma* expeditionary; avoided capture after Rebel defeat at Alegría de Pío, Dec. 1956. Rejoined Rebel Army March 24, 1957, as part of first reinforcement group (Marabuzaleros); became lieutenant in Column 6 of Second Eastern Front. Killed in battle June 26, 1958.

Sotús, Jorge (d. 1964) – Led first group of reinforcements to Rebel Army March 1957 (Marabuzaleros); captain in Rebel Army. Later broke with July 26 Movement. After victory of revolution imprisoned for counterrevolutionary activity; escaped and went to US. Killed in accident while organizing counterrevolutionary raid.

Special Period – Term used in Cuba for extremely difficult economic conditions faced during 1990s, and policies implemented to defend revolution. With fall of regimes in Eastern Europe and USSR, Cuba lost 85 percent of its foreign trade, as world capitalist crisis accelerated and economic warfare by Washington intensified. Facing deepest economic crisis since 1959, revolutionary government in 1993–94 adopted measures to address worsening conditions. By 1996, through efforts by Cuban working people, inflation was brought under control and a recovery began, although severe shortages of food and other essentials remained.

Taber, Robert (1919–1995) – US journalist; interviewed Fidel Castro for CBS-TV in Sierra Maestra 1957. Author of *M-26: The Biography of a Revolution*. An initiator of US Fair Play for Cuba Committee.

Tamayo, Leonardo (1941–) – Peasant from Sierra Maestra; joined Rebel Army mid-1957, serving in Guevara's column; member of "Suicide Squad" that took most dangerous combat missions in Column 8; accompanied Guevara to Bolivia under nom de guerre *Urbano*. Later served in internationalist missions in Nicaragua and Angola. Currently retired colonel in Ministry of the Interior.

Torres, Félix (1917–2008) – Commanded Popular Socialist Party guerrilla unit in Yaguajay, northern Las Villas 1958. Collaborated with Rebel Army column led by Camilo Cienfuegos.

Torres, Hipólito (Polo) (1929–) – Peasant from Sierra Maestra; close collaborator of Rebel Army; dubbed "Capitán Descalzo" (Captain Barefoot) by Che Guevara because of his reluctance to wear shoes.

Union of Young Communists (UJC) – Born out of Association of Rebel Youth (AJR) founded by Rebel Army Department of Instruction in Dec. 1959. Following fusion of prorevolution youth groups in Oct. 1960, AJR encompassed youth from July 26 Movement, Revolutionary Directorate, and PSP's Socialist Youth. Became UJC April 4, 1962.

UNITA (National Union for the Total Independence of Angola) – Founded 1964 to fight Portuguese colonial rule, led by Jonas Savimbi. In 1975, as Portuguese rule was collapsing, allied with apartheid South Africa and Washington in attempt to overthrow MPLA-led government of newly independent country. Over next 25 years waged war against Angolan government. Savimbi killed by government forces in Feb. 2002; UNITA signed cease-fire with Angolan government the next month.

Valdés, Ramiro (1932–) – Participated in 1953 Moncada attack, for which he was sentenced to ten years in prison. Released May 1955 following amnesty campaign. *Granma* expeditionary. Second in command of Rebel Army Column 4 in Sierra

Maestra, later becoming its commander. Second in command of Column 8 in Las Villas. Minister of interior 1961–68, 1979–85. Member of Communist Party Central Committee since 1965, Political Bureau 1965–86 and 2008 to present. One of three Sierra combatants to hold title Commander of the Revolution. Vice president of Council of State since 2009.

Viciedo, Sebastián (Pompilio) – Veteran of fight against Machado dictatorship in 1930s; volunteer in Spanish civil war. Member of Popular Socialist Party; led PSP armed unit in Sancti Spíritus area during revolutionary war. Joined Rebel Army Column 8 in Las Villas late 1958.

Villegas, Harry (1940–) – Joined Rebel Army 1957, becoming member of Columns 4 and 8 led by Che Guevara. Served with Guevara in Congo 1965 and later Bolivia under nom de guerre *Pombo*. Commanded surviving combatants who eluded encirclement by Bolivian army and returned to Cuba March 1968. Served three tours in Angola in 1970s and '80s. Commanded Border Guard brigade in 1970s. Brigadier general (retired) in FAR, member of Central Committee of Communist Party, and deputy in National Assembly. Executive vice president of Association of Combatants of the Cuban Revolution, heading its Secretariat of Patriotic-Military and Internationalist Work. Hero of the Republic of Cuba.

Youth Army of Labor (EJT) – Part of Cuba's Revolutionary Armed Forces, composed of detachments of youth who carry out agricultural, construction, and other work, as they train militarily.

Index

Acevedo, Rogelio, 96, 169
Acosta, Armando, 93, 169
Africa
   Cuito Cuanavale a milestone for, 133
   impact of Cuba on, 155
   imperialist exploitation of, 149–50
   See also Angola; Angola: Cuban mission in; Battles: Angola; South Africa
Agrarian reform, 78, 101–2
   bonds (compensation), 164–65
   and expropriation of United Fruit Company, 163–67
   as "indispensable" (Fidel Castro), 165
   "revolution crossed Rubicon" (Raúl Castro), 102
   See also Farmers; Landowners, large
Agriculture
   See Citrus farming; Farmers; Farmers markets; Sugar industry; Sugar workers; Youth Army of Labor (EJT)
Agriculture, Ministry of, 116
Aguirrechu, Iraida, 20
Alayón, Pelayo, 104–5, 169
Aldabonazo (Armando Hart), 10
Almeida, Juan, 54, 169–70
   at battle of El Uvero (May 28, 1957), 76–77
   leadership qualities of, 84
Altos de Conrado, 78
Álvarez, Miguel, 96, 170

Alves, Nito, 170
   leads coup attempt (1977), 143–44
Ambriz, 138
Ambrizete, battle of (Jan. 1976), 138
Ameijeiras, Efigenio, 76, 170
Ammunition
   See Weapons
Amnesty campaign, after 1953 Moncada attack, 54, 59
Angola
   Congress of Berlin and (1885), 149
   coup attempt (1977), 143–46
   deaths of Angolans during war against South Africa, 132
   imperialist exploitation of, 149–50
   mercenaries in, 138–39
   Ministry of Interior, 145
   north, liberation of (1976), 139
   Portugal, independence from (1975), 129–31, 142
   South Africa and, 27, 129–43, 145, 147–48, 154
   US imperialism and, 14, 129–43, 147
   wealth of, oil and mineral, 130, 142, 146, 150
   Zaire and, 14–15, 130, 138, 141
   See also Battles: Angola; Cabinda; FAPLA; FNLA; MPLA; UNITA
Angola: Cuban mission in, 14–16, 27, 129–59
   attempted coup and (1977), 14–15, 143–46

191

Cabinda, 14, 149–53
civilian collaborators, 27, 129, 143, 145, 148–49, 151
Cuban casualties, 14, 133, 136
Cuban Five and, 153–57
Fidel Castro's leadership of, 136, 138, 147–48
historic place of, 130–31, 156–58
logistics of, 147–49
popular character of, 14–15, 129, 131, 133, 148, 156
as "refuge" of voluntary labor, 157
relations with Angolan government, 145–46
size and duration, 14, 129, 133, 143, 147–48, 151, 157
Soviet Union and, 131, 146, 151
strengthened Cuban Revolution, 15, 153–59
volunteers, medical, 151–52
Youth Army of Labor and, 122
Army, Batista
air attacks by, 84
casualties, 77–78, 80, 92
declining morale, 93
dismantlement of, 13, 103–4
execution of Rebel Army prisoners, 88
"final offensive" by, 26, 55, 81–83
repression against farmers, 79–80
response to Nov. 1956 uprising, 61
spies, 84
Arroba, defined, 41
Arroyo del Infierno, battle of (Jan. 22, 1957), 82
Art Daily, 168
Artemisa, 80
Art Info, 168
Association of Combatants of the Cuban Revolution, 20, 27, 125, 170
Authentic Organization, 25, 57, 59, 170
Authentic Party, 57, 170–71

Babún timber company, 76

Bagasse, 36
Baker, John, 139
Barnes, Jack, 10
Batey (sugar company town), 33, 39
Batista, Fulgencio, 171
attempted assassination of (1957), 55
coup by (1952), 25, 53
flight from Cuba (Jan. 1, 1959), 26, 56, 98
Batista regime
bourgeois opposition to, 53
character of, 33, 53–54
collapse of, 13, 26, 56, 99
and *Guardia Rural* (rural police), 13, 49, 59–60, 64
and Military Intelligence Service (SIM), 66
repression by, 49, 54, 57
resistance by working people, 9, 47–49, 53, 57, 59
and US criminals, 33
See also Army, Batista; Tribunals, revolutionary
Battles: Angola
Caporolo (Nov. 1975), 136
Nambuangongo (Dec. 1975), 137
Quitexe (Jan. 1976), 138
Carmona (Jan. 1976), 137–38
Ambrizete (Jan. 1976), 138
San Antonio do Zaire (Feb. 1976), 135–37, 139
Cangamba (Aug. 1983), 143
Cuito Cuanavale (Dec. 1987–Mar. 1988), 132–33, 143, 148
Battles: Cuba
La Plata (Jan. 17, 1957), 82
Arroyo del Infierno (Jan. 22, 1957), 82
El Uvero (May 28, 1957), 26, 75–77, 80, 82
Che Guevara on, 75–76
Bueycito (Aug. 11, 1957), 78
Palma Mocha (Aug. 20, 1957), 82
El Hombrito (Aug. 29, 1957), 78
Mar Verde (Nov. 29, 1957), 80

INDEX

Cuatro Compañeros (Sept. 14, 1958), 87
Güinía de Miranda (Oct. 26–27, 1958), 90–91
Santa Lucía (Dec. 3, 1958), 92
Fomento (Dec. 15–18, 1958), 92
Cabaiguán (Dec. 23, 1958), 92
Placetas (Dec. 23, 1958), 92–93
Remedios (Dec. 26, 1958), 92–93
Caibarién (Dec. 26, 1958), 92–93
Yaguajay, 91, 93, 95
Santa Clara (Dec. 29, 1958–Jan. 1, 1959), 26, 56, 93–98
Bayamo, 54, 65, 82
Bay of Pigs (Playa Girón) (1961), 103, 107
Bermúdez, Alcibíades, 57, 59, 171
"Black Carlota," 131
Blacks, discrimination against, 32, 101, 167, 174
Bohemia magazine, 21
Bordón, Víctor, 89, 92–93, 171
Boston Globe, 168
Buda (trolley), 43
Bueycito, battle of (Aug. 11, 1957), 78

Cabaiguán, battle of (Dec. 23, 1958), 92
Caballete de Casa school for Rebel Army recruits, 93
Cabinda, 14, 27, 130, 141–42, 149–53
 agriculture and barter in, 153
 colonial plunder of, 149–50
 Congress of Berlin (1885) and, 149
 development, level of, 152–53
 food imports, 152–53
 forestry in, 151
 Gulf Oil in, 150
 tribes in, 150
 women, condition of, 153
Cabinda Enclave Liberation Front
 See FLEC
Caetano, Jacobo (Monstruo Inmortal) [Immortal Monster], 144, 171
Caibarién, battle of (Dec. 26, 1958), 92–93

Calero, Róger, 20
"Callan, Colonel," 139
Camacho, Julio, 108, 171
Camagüey province, 118
 Guevara's column in, 84–88
Camajuaní, 95
Cangamba, battle of (Aug. 1983), 143
Cape Verde, 129, 142
"Capitan Descalzo" (Captain Barefoot), 81
Caporolo, battle of (Nov. 1975), 136
Caracas Peak, 71
Carmona, battle of (Jan. 1976), 137–38
Carreira, Iko, 139, 171–72
Casillas Lumpuy, Joaquín, 98, 172
Castellanos, Alberto, 103, 172
Castro, Fidel, 14, 47, 53–54, 57, 59, 172
 on agrarian reform as "indispensable," 165
 on Angola, 131, 142, 146
 Angolan mission, leadership of, 136, 138, 147–48
 on campaign for ten million tons of sugar, 114
 on collapse of Soviet Union, 15
 Column 1, as commander of, 70–71, 75
 El Uvero, in battle of, 76
 qualities of, 75, 125
 on revolutionary tribunals, 19, 105, 107
 Special Period, on building monument to, 123
 and United Fruit Company, 164
 on voluntary labor, 157
Castro, Raúl, 54, 76, 108–9, 172–73
 agrarian reform, revolution "crossed Rubicon," 102
 on Angola, 15, 157
 on Fidel Castro's qualities, 75
 leadership qualities of, 84
 on youth, challenges to, 126
Castro Mercader, Raúl, 60, 62, 66, 173
Cayo Juan Claro, 38
Cayo Probado, 71

Central Highway, 167
Changada, 139
Chaparra sugar mill (now Jesús Menéndez), 25, 33, 36, 101
Chibás, Eduardo, 53
Chinese, in Cuba, 32, 166
Chiquita Brands International, 164
See also United Fruit Company
Chomón, Faure, 56, 91, 173
Choy, Armando, 10
Chui, Gustavo, 10
Ciego de Ávila, 93
Cienfuegos, Camilo, 54, 173
 as commander in Escambray, 56, 91, 93, 95
 as commander in Sierra, 82–83
 leadership qualities of, 82–83
 sense of humor of, 84
 Yaguajay, in battle of, 91, 93, 95
Cien horas con Fidel (One Hundred Hours with Fidel) (Ignacio Ramonet), 19, 107
Citrus farming, 107, 121, 124
Ciudad Deportiva, 104
Colombia (Las Tunas province), 118
Colomé, Abelardo (Furry), 136, 173–74
Colonos, 33, 36, 40–43, 174
 in battle over sugar "differential," 46–47
 debt to sugar companies and, 41, 43
 hired labor of, 45
 and sugar quota, 41–42
Committees for the Defense of the Revolution (CDRs), 115, 118, 120, 174
Company stores, 11, 39, 41
Congo, Belgian colony of, 129, 149
Congo, Democratic Republic of
 See Zaire
Congo, Republic of
 See Congo-Brazzaville
Congo-Brazzaville, 130, 137, 150–53
Congo River, 139
Congress of Berlin (1885), 149
Corrales, Raúl, 20–21, 163, 167–68

Costa Rica, 164
Crespo, Luis, 76, 174
Cristino Naranjo sugar mill, 112
CTC (Confederation of Cuban Workers), 115, 174–75
Cuando Cubango, 143
Cuatro Compañeros, battle of (Sept. 14, 1958), 87
Cuba
 Cuba Técnica (agency), 148–49
 independence wars in (1868–1898), 31, 83, 87, 166
 labor shortage in, 36, 124
 military service in, 121
 Ministry of Foreign Investment and Economic Collaboration, 149
 Ministry of Foreign Relations, 149
 Ministry of Interior, 14, 156
 "pseudorepublic" imposed by US, 31
 revolution of 1933, 36
 slave rebellion (1843), 131
 social conditions, before revolution, 10–12, 31–33, 40, 159, 165, 167
 Territorial Troop Militia, 157
 US imperialist domination of, 31–32
 voluntary labor in, 109–10, 118–20, 157–58
 See also Farmers; Sugar industry; Sugar workers
Cuba and the Coming American Revolution (Jack Barnes), 10
"Cuba in Revolution" (photo exhibition, 2010), 167–68
Cubana Airlines, 156
Cuban-American Sugar Mills Co., 10, 33, 38–39
 attack on powder magazine of, 25, 54–55, 60–63
Cuban Communist Party
 Agriculture Department of, 116–17
 political responsibilities, 115–16

INDEX

See also Ten million tons of sugar, campaign for (1970); Zayas, Luis Alfonso, responsibilities after 1959
Cuban Five, 153–57
Cuban independence wars (1868–1898), 31, 83, 87
Cuban Revolution
  as example, 126, 155
  fight to overthrow dictatorship, 9, 53–98
  immediate measures by, 18–19, 101–3, 163, 166
  proletarian character of, 9–10, 19–21, 168
  rectification process in, 119, 184
  role of youth in, 9–10, 126
  Special Period in, 15–17, 122–23, 187
  Youth Army of Labor and, 16–17, 120–22, 124
  See also Agrarian reform; Cuban Five; Rebel Army; Revolutionary Armed Forces
Cuba's Internationalist Foreign Policy (Fidel Castro), 14
Cuba Técnica, 148–49
Cuito Cuanavale, battle of (Dec.1987–Mar. 1988), 132–33, 143, 147–48

"Dead time," 11, 32, 38, 102
de la Fe, Ernesto, 104, 175
Delicias sugar mill (now Antonio Guiteras), 33, 36, 65, 101
"Democratic" counterrevolution, US-instigated, 18
Díaz, Epifanio, 70, 175
Díaz, Julio, 76, 80
Domínguez, Guillermo, 57, 59–61, 64–65, 175
Dreke, Víctor, 10

El Cobre, 65
Electrification extended, 102
El Hombrito, 81
  battle of (Aug. 29, 1957), 78

El Uvero, battle of (May 28, 1957), 26, 75–77, 80
Episodes of the Cuban Revolutionary War (Ernesto Che Guevara), 10
Equatorial Guinea, 150
Escambray mountains, 13
  counterrevolutionary bands in, 103
  guerrilla groups in, 55–56, 88–92
  See also Las Villas campaign; Revolutionary Directorate; Second National Front of the Escambray
Espín, Vilma, 70, 175
Evaristo, Eduardo (Bakaloff), 144, 175

FAPLA (Popular Armed Forces for the Liberation of Angola), 27, 135–39, 143–46, 150, 175
  and Cuito Cuanavale, 132–33, 143, 148
Farmers
  Batista army repression against, 79–80
  Cuban Revolution and, 101–2
  Rebel Army and, 75, 78–79
  social conditions of, pre-1959, 11, 31–32, 165
  United Fruit Company and, 163–67
  See also Agrarian reform
Farmers markets, 122, 124
Fernández, José Ramón, 108, 176
Fernández Mell, Oscar, 103, 176
Fernández Monte de Oca, Alberto (Pacho), 97, 176
FLEC (Cabinda Enclave Liberation Front), 141, 150, 176
FMC (Federation of Cuban Women), 115, 175–76
FNLA (Angolan National Liberation Front), 137–38, 142, 176–77
  mercenaries and, 138–39
  South Africa and, 130, 135
  support for, in north, 141

Zaire and, 133, 141
  See also Roberto, Holden
Fomento, battle of (Dec. 15–18, 1958), 92
Foreign Investment and Economic Collaboration, Ministry of, 149
Forestry, 27, 107, 151
France, 153
Freedom Caravan (Jan. 1959), 57
Frías, Ciro, 70, 177
From the Escambray to the Congo (Víctor Dreke), 10

García, Armando, 64, 177
García, Calixto, 76, 177
García, Guillermo, 74, 77, 177
García, Rigoberto, 27, 124, 177
García Márquez, Gabriel, 130–31
Gavilanes, 93
Gómez, Máximo, 87, 177–78
Gómez Ochoa, Delio, 55, 178
González, Fernando, 154–55
  See also Cuban Five
González, René, 154–55
  on "giving history a little shove," 154
  See also Cuban Five
Granma landing (Dec. 1956), 25–26, 61
  support actions for, 54–55, 60–64
Granma newspaper, 21
Grau, Ricardo José, 104, 178
Grau San Martín, Ramón, 104, 178
Guáimaro, 119
Guardia Rural (rural police), 13, 60, 64
  as strike breakers, 49
Guatemala, 164, 166
Guayos, 93
Guerra Matos, Felipe (Guerrita), 66, 70, 178
Guerrero, Antonio, 154
  See also Cuban Five
Guevara, Ernesto Che, 10, 18, 55, 76, 178
  Africa trip (1965), 129
  on Batista army's "final offensive," 83

  Column 4, as commander of, 26, 77
  Column 8, as commander of, 13, 26, 55–56, 83, 89–91, 93
  Congo, mission in (1965), 129
  leadership qualities of, 78–79, 82–84, 88
  Marabuzalero reinforcements and, 70–71, 74
  as "toothpuller," 78–79
  on voluntary labor, 157
Guevara, Ernesto Che, in battles
  El Uvero (May 28, 1957), 76
  Güinia de Miranda (Oct. 26–27, 1958), 90–91
  Santa Clara (Dec. 29, 1958–Jan. 1, 1959), 93–97
  Yaguajay, 95
Guinea-Bissau, 129, 142
Güinía de Miranda, battle of (Oct. 26–27, 1958), 90–91
Guiteras, Antonio, 36, 179
Gulf Oil, 150
Gutiérrez Menoyo, Eloy, 88, 179

Haiti, Cuban volunteers in, 12
Hart, Armando, 10, 67, 179
Havana, entry into (Jan. 1959), 57, 91, 98, 103
Havana province, 87
Health care, 32, 102
Hernández, Gerardo, 153–55
  "Angola was a school," 155
  See also Cuban Five
Hernández, Hernando, 104, 179
Holguín, 26, 39, 65, 82, 108–16, 163
Hotel Cloris (Santa Clara), 95, 97–98
Hotel Presidente (Luanda), 145
Housing, 118–20, 167
How Far We Slaves Have Come! (Nelson Mandela, Fidel Castro), 14
Hussein, Saddam, 20

Iglesias, Joel, 81, 179
Infant mortality, prior to 1959, 32
Informers, 84

INRA (National Institute of Agrarian Reform), 163–64, 166–67
International Center of Photography (New York), 167
Internationalist missions
 Rebel Army as moral foundation of, 13–14
 as "refuge" of voluntary labor, 157
 strengthen revolution, 12, 16, 153–71
 See also Angola: Cuban mission in
Isle of Pines
 See Isle of Youth
Isle of Youth, 59, 107

Jíbaro, 84, 87
Júcaro-Morón line, 85, 87
July 26 Movement, 180
 formation of (1955), 54
 Popular Socialist Party and, 55, 91
 Revolutionary Directorate and, 55, 91
July 26 Movement, *Llano* (urban underground)
 armed actions by, 25, 54–55, 59–63
 in Puerto Padre, 12, 25, 45–46, 54–55, 57, 59–63
 Rebel Army, supply lines to, 70, 75
 and reinforcements, 12, 26, 55, 64, 66–67, 70
 in Santiago de Cuba, 54
 Zayas joins, 25, 59

Koppel, Martín, 20
Korda, Alberto, 168

Labañino, Ramon, 154
 See also Cuban Five
La Cabaña fortress, 18, 26, 98, 103–4
La Mesa, 81
Landowners, large
 expropriation of, 101, 163–67

extent of holdings, 31–32, 164
La Plata, battle of (Jan. 17, 1957), 82
Lara, Lúcio, 139, 180
Las Mercedes, 81
Las Parras, 39
Las Tunas, 38–39, 46, 82
Las Tunas province, 25, 27, 33, 117–20
 building housing in, 118–20
 building roads in, 117–18
 Zayas as Communist Party secretary in, 117–20
Las Villas campaign, 26, 55–56, 82–83, 88–98
 See also Escambray mountains
Life expectancy, prior to 1959, 32
Literacy, prior to 1959, 32, 102
Lobo, Julio, 49, 180
Luanda, 130–31, 133, 135–36, 139, 144–45, 149, 152

Maceo, Antonio, 83, 87, 180
Machado, Gerardo, 19
Malanga, 153
Malaria, 32
Mambises, 166
Manatí, 38
Mandela, Nelson, 14, 133
Mantua, 83
Manzanillo, 61, 64, 66–67, 81, 98
Marabuzaleros (Rebel Army reinforcements), 12, 26, 55, 64, 66–67, 70–71, 74–75
March 13 Revolutionary Directorate
 See Revolutionary Directorate
Marianas in Combat (Teté Puebla), 10
Mariel-Majana line, 87
Martínez Rosales, Alberto (Kiko), 97, 181
Mar Verde, battle of (Nov. 29, 1957), 80
Marx, Karl, 9
Matanzas, 108
Matanzas province, 131
Matos, Huber, 181
Matthews, Herbert, 66, 70, 181
Mayarí, 163

M'banza Congo, 139
Mbridge River, 138
Menéndez, Jesús, 33–34, 98, 181
Mercenaries (in Angola), 138–39
Mexico, Cuban revolutionaries in, 54
Militant newspaper, 168
Military Intelligence Service (SIM), 66
Military service (in Cuba), 121–22
Minas del Frío school for Rebel Army recruits, 81
Minibrigades, 119
Ministry of Interior (Cuba), 14, 156
Miret, Pedro, 66, 181
"Missile" Crisis (Oct. 1962), 103, 108
Mobutu Sese Seko, 130, 141, 181
  See also Zaire
Moncada attack (1953), 53–54, 57
Moracén, Rafael, 145, 182
Morales, Calixto, 76, 182
Morejón, Pedro, 104–5, 182
Morgan, William, 88, 182
Mozambique, 129, 142
MPLA (Popular Movement for the Liberation of Angola), 182
  attempted coup by "microfaction," 14–15, 143–46
  Cuba's support for, 135
  as leading force in struggle for independence, 130, 135
  Political Bureau, 144
  and Soviet Union, 130–31, 146, 149
  support for, in central Angola, 141
"M-26" rockets, 78
Mussolini, Benito, 19–20

Nambuangongo, battle of (Dec. 1975), 137
National Association of Small Farmers (ANAP), 115, 182
Netherlands, 153
Neto, Agostinho, 15, 145, 182
  appeal for Cuban aid, 130, 135
  attempted coup against, 143–46
  presidential regiment of, 145
New York Times, 66, 138, 168
Nicaragua, 164
Noval, Liborio, 168
Núñez Jiménez, Antonio, 103, 164, 167, 182–83
N'zeto, 138

October "Missile" Crisis (1962), 103, 108
Operation Carlota, 131, 136
  See also Angola: Cuban mission in
Oriente province, 33
  Rebel Army combat in, 54–57, 67–82
Orthodox Party, 53–54
Our History Is Still Being Written (Armando Choy, Gustavo Chui, Moisés Sío Wong), 10, 14

País, Frank, 59, 64, 183
  murder of (1957), 74
  and 1956 uprising, 54, 60–61
  as organizer of reinforcements, 67
Palma Mocha, battle of (Aug. 20, 1957), 82
Panama, 164
Pardo Guerra, Ramón, 93, 95
Paris Commune (1871)
  Karl Marx on, 9
Pedrero, 92
Pedrero Pact, 91
Pena, Félix, 76, 183
People's Power (municipal government), 118
Pérez, Adriana, 154
Pérez, Cresencio, 74, 76, 183
Philippines, 31
Pinar del Río, 82–83, 108
Pinar Quemado, 78
Pioneers (Angola), 144
Placetas, battle of (Dec. 23, 1958), 92–93
Playa Girón (Bay of Pigs) (1961), 103, 107–8

INDEX

Pointe-Noire, 151–53
Pombo: A Man of Che's 'guerrilla' (Harry Villegas), 10
Popular Movement for the Liberation of Angola
 See MPLA
Popular Socialist Party (Cuba), 56, 89, 91, 183–84
Porto Amboim, 133
Portugal, 129–30, 135, 138, 141, 149–50, 152
Preston sugar mill (now Guatemala), 163–67
Prío Socarrás, Carlos, 53, 57, 184
Puebla, Teté, 10
Puerto Padre, 25, 33, 46, 70, 101, 118
 attack on powder magazine in, 25, 54–55, 59–64
 isolation of, 39
 July 26 movement in, 12, 25, 46, 54–55, 57, 59–64
 working class in, 47, 49
Puerto Rico, 31
Pupo Peña, Orlando, 60, 62, 64, 66, 184

Quibala, 133
Quifangondo, 135
Quitexe, battle of (Jan. 1976), 138

Radio Rebelde, 78
Ramonet, Ignacio, 19, 107
Ramos Latour, René, 74, 184
Rebel Army
 becomes Revolutionary Armed Forces, 13, 103
 casualty figures, 77–78, 91
 deaths of leading cadres, 59–60, 74, 80, 96
 farmers, agricultural workers, support to, 12–13, 75
 Havana, Santiago de Cuba, occupied by, 56–57
 interviews in US press, 66
 leadership development in, 82–84
 as moral foundation of Revolutionary Armed Forces, internationalist missions, 13–14
 recruitment to, 77
 reinforcements to, 12, 26, 55, 64, 66–67, 70
 resists Batista "final offensive," 55, 81–82
 schools for recruits, 78, 81, 93
 size of, 55, 70–71, 74, 77, 96–97
 strategy and tactics, 83, 92–93
 supply lines, 70, 75–76
 Tactical Force of, 107
 westward march (1958), 13, 55, 82, 84–88
 Zayas in, 26, 70–98
Rebel Army columns and fronts
 Column 1 (Fidel Castro), 70–77
 Column 2 (Camilo Cienfuegos)
  march westward (1958), 55
  Yaguajay front, 91, 93, 95
  march on Havana, 56–57
 Column 4 (Che Guevara, Ramiro Valdés), 26, 81
 Column 8 (Che Guevara), 13, 26, 80–91
 Second Front (Raúl Castro), 55, 84
 Third Front (Juan Almeida, Calixto García), 55, 84
Rectification process, 119, 184
Redondo, Ciro, 71, 76, 80–81, 184–85
Remedios, battle of (Dec. 26, 1958), 92–93
Revolutionary Armed Forces (FAR), 13, 103, 185
 education in, 108, 121–22
 Youth Army of Labor (EJT) and, 16–17, 120–22
 Zayas in, 101–8, 125, 133–39
 See also Angola: Cuban mission in; Rebel Army
Revolutionary Directorate, 55–56, 89, 91, 95–96, 185
Revolutionary National Militia, 14, 103
Revolutionary National Police, 14, 103

Road building, 45–46, 117–18, 167
Roberto, Holden, 130, 133, 135, 137, 185
  CIA and, 141
  Mobutu Sese Seko and, 141
  See also FNLA
Rodríguez, Roberto (Vaquerito), 93, 96, 185
Rodríguez Robles, Francisco, 21

Sabanazo, 39
Sabotage of Batista regime, 59–60
Salanueva, Olga, 154
Salas, Osvaldo, 168
San Antonio do Zaire, battle of (Feb. 1976), 135–37, 139
Sánchez, Celia, 66–67, 77, 185–86
Sánchez, Universo, 76, 186
Sánchez Mosquera, Ángel, 79–81, 186
Sancti Spiritus, 93, 119
San Salvador province (Angola), 139
Santa Clara, 107
Santa Clara, battle of (Dec. 29, 1958–Jan. 1, 1959), 26, 56, 93–98
Santa Lucía, battle of (Dec. 3, 1958), 92
Santiago de Cuba, 54, 57, 64–67
  rebel encirclement of, 56, 83, 93
  supply network for Rebel Army and, 70, 75–76
  underground struggle in, 60–61
Santo Domingo (Las Villas province), 93, 98
Savimbi, Jonas, 130, 135, 186
  See also UNITA
Schools for Rebel Army recruits, 78, 81, 93
Schueg, Víctor, 138–39, 186
Second National Front of the Escambray, 88–91, 186
  hatred of farmers for, 56
Sierra Maestra mountains, 12–13, 70–84
Sío Wong, Moisés, 10
Slavery, 32, 166
Sosa, Merob, 104, 187
Sosa Blanco, Jesús, 104, 187
Sotto, Pedro, 76, 187

Sotús, Jorge, 76, 187
South Africa
  and Angola, invasion of, 14, 16, 27, 129–43, 147
  Cuito Cuanavale, defeat in battle of, 132–33, 143, 147
Soviet Union
  Angola and, 131, 146, 149, 151
  Cuba's economic relations with, 15–16, 109, 114
  disintegration of, 15, 123, 126
Soyo, 135
Spain, 31, 87, 166
"Spanish-American War," 31
Special Period, 15–17, 122–23, 187
  Fidel Castro on building monument to, 123
"Sputniks," 78
State Department (US), 165
Sugar industry, prior to 1959, 10–11, 36, 38
  batey (company town), 33, 39
  battle over "differential," 46–49
  company stores, 11, 33, 39, 41
  Cuban-American Sugar Mills Co. and, 33, 38–39
  "dead time," 11, 32, 38, 102
  employment in, 36, 38
  Lobo, Julio and, 49, 180
  quota assigned by United States, 11, 41, 164, 166
  quota system for *colonos*, 11, 41–42
  railroads and, 11, 38–39
  reliance on hand labor, 36
  and road brigades, 39, 46
  US control of, 10–11, 31
  wages in, 36
  See also Sugar workers; Ten million tons, campaign for (1970)
Sugar industry, after 1959
  in Las Tunas province, 120
  mechanization of, 110
  need for labor in, 110, 121
  See also Ten million tons, campaign for; United Fruit Company

See also Ten million tons, campaign for; United Fruit Company
Sugar mills
 Chaparra (now Jesús Menéndez), 25, 33, 36, 101
 Cristino Naranjo, 112
 Delicias (now Antonio Guiteras), 33, 36, 65, 101
 Preston (now Guatemala), 163–64, 166–67
 Triunvirato, 131
Sugar workers, 36, 38
 combativity of, 10–11, 49
 mechanization, fight against, 49
 strike by (1955), 47–49
"Suicide Squad," 96
Supply lines, for Rebel Army, 70, 75–76

Taber, Robert, 66–67, 187
Tamayo, Leonardo, 103, 188
Ten million tons of sugar, campaign for (1970), 109–16
 assessment of, 111–17
 importance of, 109, 114
 preparations for, 110–12, 115
Territorial Troop Militia, 157
Torres, Félix, 91, 188
Torres, Hipólito (Polo, "Captain Barefoot"), 81, 188
Tribunals, revolutionary, 18–20, 26, 101, 104–5, 107
 Fidel Castro on "justice, not vengeance," 19, 105
Triunvirato sugar mill, 131
Tuberculosis, 32

Unemployment, prior to 1959, 22, 26, 28
Union of Young Communists (UJC), 188
 Youth Army of Labor (EJT) and, 120
UNITA (National Union for the Total Independence of Angola), 149, 188
 FLEC and, 150
 South Africa and, 130, 132, 135, 141, 143
 stronghold of, in south, 141, 143
 United States and, 135, 141
 Zaire and, 141
United Fruit Company, 10, 20–21
 expropriation of by revolutionary government, 163–67
United Nations, 165–66
United States imperialism
 Angola war and, 14, 129–32, 135, 141–43, 147
 class blindness of, 14
 Costa Rica and, 164
 Cuba, domination by, prior to 1959, 10–11, 31–32, 166
 Cuba, economic and political war against, 17–19, 165–66
 Guatemala and, 164
 Iraq and, 19–20
 Jim Crow segregation, imported to Cuba by, 32, 167
 Nicaragua and, 164
 Panama and, 164
 Philippines and, 31
 promotes "democratic" counterrevolution in Cuba, 18
 Puerto Rico and, 31

Valdés, Ramiro, 25, 54, 71, 76, 80, 93, 188–89
Vaquerito, 93, 96, 185
Velasco, 39
Venezuela, Cuban volunteers in, 12, 158
Viciedo, Pompilio, 91, 189
Villegas, Harry, 10, 20, 103, 189
Voluntary labor, 109–10, 118–20, 157–58

Weapons
 in Angola, 135, 138, 146
 Batista army superiority in, 76, 80
 captured from Batista army, 63, 78, 80, 82, 91–93

INDEX

Women, condition of
 in Angola, 153
 in Cuba, prior to 1959, 32–33
 in Cuba, after 1959, 102, 115
Workers: agricultural, 10–11, 32, 110, 163–64, 167
 support to Rebel Army by, 75

Yaguajay, battle of, 91, 93, 95
Youth, 53–54, 115, 120–22, 126
Youth Army of Labor (EJT), 16–17, 27, 120–22, 124, 189

Zaire, 139, 150, 153
 as Belgian colony, 129, 149
 FNLA, UNITA and, 15, 138, 141
 US imperialism and, 130
Zambia, 150
Zayas, Luis Alfonso, 20–21
 childhood and youth, 25–26, 33, 36, 43–46, 57–74
 in Authentic Organization, 57
 in July 26 Movement, 25, 45, 59–70
 attack on powder magazine in Puerto Padre, 12, 25, 54–55, 60–64
 Rebel Army, combatant in, 12, 26, 70–98
 in defeat of Batista "final offensive," 26
 in march to Las Villas (1958), 26, 84–88
 ranks held in Rebel Army and Revolutionary Armed Forces, 26, 27, 78, 87, 108
Zayas, Luis Alfonso, in battles
 El Uvero (May 28, 1957), 26, 76–77
 Bueycito (August 11, 1957), 78
 El Hombrito (Aug. 29, 1957), 78
 Güinía de Miranda (Oct. 26–27, 1958), 90–91
 Santa Lucía (Dec. 3, 1958), 92
 Fomento (Dec. 15–18, 1958), 92
 Cabaiguán (Dec. 23, 1958), 92
 Placetas (Dec. 23, 1958), 92
 Remedios (Dec. 26, 1958), 92
 Santa Clara (Dec. 29, 1958–Jan. 1, 1959), 93–98
Zayas, Luis Alfonso, responsibilities after 1959, 14
 in charge of prisoners from Batista regime (1959), 18, 26, 104–7
 participant in revolutionary tribunals (1959), 105
 in Rebel Army Tactical Force, Santa Clara (1959), 107
 reforestation, Isle of Pines (1960–61), 107–8
 Basic Course for officers (1961), 108
 chief of staff, combat unit defending Havana (1962), 108
 director, political section, Western Army (1962–67), 108
 member Communist Party Central Committee (1965–86), 26
 Advanced Course for officers (1967), 108
 commander, Revolutionary Armed Forces (1967), 108
 Communist Party secretary in Holguín (1968–72), 108–16
 Central Committee Agriculture Department, Havana province (1972–75), 116–17
 Angola, internationalist mission in (1975–76), 27, 117, 133–39
 Angola, internationalist mission in (1977–78), 27, 143–49
 in Youth Army of Labor (1978–80, 1987–98), 16–17, 27, 120–22, 124–25
 Communist Party secretary in Las Tunas (1980–85), 117–20
 Angola, internationalist mission in (1985–87), 14, 27, 149–53
 Association of Combatants of the Cuban Revolution (2000–), 27, 125

from Pathfinder

MALCOLM X, BLACK LIBERATION AND THE ROAD TO WORKERS POWER

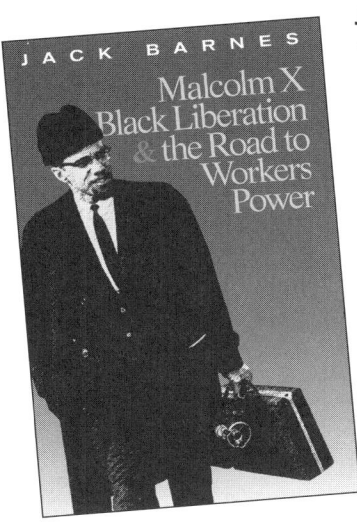

JACK BARNES

"Don't start with Blacks as an oppressed nationality. Start with the vanguard place of workers who are Black in broad, proletarian-led struggles in the US. From the Civil War to today, the historical record is mind-boggling. It's the strength and resilience, not the oppression, that bowls you over."—*Jack Barnes*

Drawing lessons from a century and a half of struggle, this book helps us understand why the revolutionary conquest of power by the working class will make possible the final battle for Black freedom—and open the way to a world based not on exploitation, violence, and racism, but human solidarity. A socialist world.

$20. Also in Spanish and French.

Companion volume to

THE CHANGING FACE OF U.S. POLITICS

Working-Class Politics and the Trade Unions

JACK BARNES

A handbook for working people seeking to build the kind of party needed to prepare for coming class battles through which we will revolutionize ourselves, our unions, and all society.

$24. Also in Spanish, French, and Swedish.

WWW.PATHFINDERPRESS.COM

Class Struggle in the United States

Is Socialist Revolution in the U.S. Possible?
A Necessary Debate
MARY-ALICE WATERS

"To think a socialist revolution in the U.S. is not possible, you'd have to believe not only that the wealthy ruling families and their economic wizards have found a way to 'manage' capitalism. You'd have to close your eyes to the spreading imperialist wars and economic, financial, and social crises we are in the midst of." —Mary-Alice Waters.

In talks given as part of a wide-ranging debate at the 2007 and 2008 Venezuela Book Fairs, Waters explains why a socialist revolution is not only possible, but why revolutionary struggles by working people are inevitable— battles forced on us by the rulers' crisis-driven assaults on our living and job conditions, on our very humanity. $7. Also in Spanish, French, and Swedish.

Cuba and the Coming American Revolution
JACK BARNES

The Cuban Revolution of 1959 had a worldwide political impact, including on working people and youth in the U.S. In the early 1960s, says Barnes, "the mass proletarian-based struggle to bring down Jim Crow segregation in the South was marching toward bloody victories as the Cuban Revolution was advancing." The deep-going social transformation Cuban toilers fought for and won set an example that socialist revolution is not only necessary—it can be made and defended by workers and farmers in the imperialist heartland as well. Foreword by Mary-Alice Waters. $10. Also in Spanish and French.

www.pathfinderpress.com

Teamster Rebellion
FARRELL DOBBS
The first of a four-volume participant's account of how strikes and organizing drives across the Midwest in the 1930s, initiated by leaders of Teamsters Local 574 in Minneapolis, paved the way for industrial unions and a fighting working-class social movement. These battles showed what workers and farmers can achieve when they have the leadership they deserve. Dobbs was a central part of that class-struggle leadership. $19. Also in Spanish, French, and Swedish.

Fighting Racism in World War II
From the Pages of the 'Militant'
An account from 1939 to 1945 of struggles against racism and lynch-mob terror in face of patriotic appeals to postpone resistance until after U.S. "victory" in World War II. These struggles—of a piece with anti-imperialist battles the world over—helped lay the basis for the mass Black rights movement in the 1950s and '60s. $25

The First Ten Years of American Communism
JAMES P. CANNON
A founding leader of the communist movement in the U.S. recounts early efforts to build a proletarian party emulating the Bolshevik leadership of the October 1917 revolution in Russia. $22

Revolutionary Continuity
Marxist Leadership in the U.S.
FARRELL DOBBS
How successive generations of fighters joined in struggles that shaped the U.S. labor movement, seeking to build a revolutionary leadership able to advance the interests of workers and small farmers and link up with fellow toilers worldwide. 2 vols. *The Early Years: 1848-1917*, $20; *Birth of the Communist Movement: 1918-1922*, $19

The Cuban Revolution and

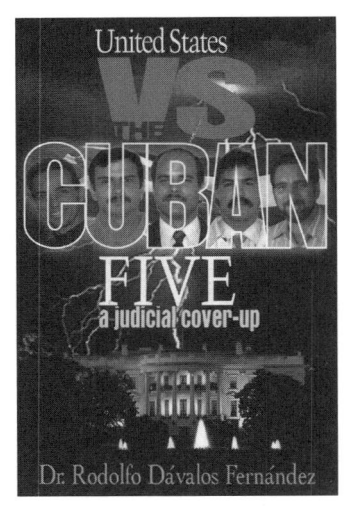

United States vs. The Cuban Five
A Judicial Cover-up
Rodolfo Dávalos Fernández
Held in U.S. prisons since 1998, five Cuban revolutionists were framed up for being part of a "Cuban spy network" in Florida. They were keeping tabs for Cuban government on rightist groups with a long record of armed attacks on Cuba from U.S. soil. "From start to finish," says the author, court proceedings were "tainted, corrupt, and vindictive. Every right to 'due process of law' was flouted." $22. Also in Spanish.

Episodes of the Cuban Revolutionary War, 1956–58
Ernesto Che Guevara
A firsthand account of the political events and military campaigns that culminated in the January 1959 popular insurrection that overthrew the US-backed dictatorship in Cuba. With clarity and humor, Guevara describes his own political education. He explains how the struggle transformed the men and women of the Rebel Army and July 26 Movement, opening the door to the first socialist revolution in the Americas. $30

Marianas in Combat
Teté Puebla and the Mariana Grajales Women's Platoon in Cuba's Revolutionary War 1956–58
Teté Puebla
Brigadier General Teté Puebla joined the struggle to overthrow the U.S.-backed Batista dictatorship in Cuba in 1956, at age fifteen. This is her story—from clandestine action in the cities, to officer in the Rebel Army's first all-women's platoon. The fight to transform the social and economic status of women is inseparable from Cuba's socialist revolution. $14. Also in Spanish.

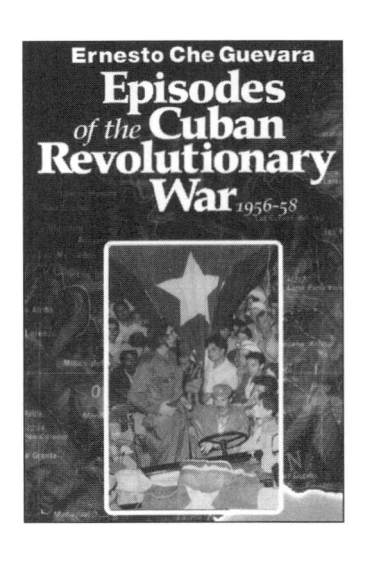

World Politics

Our History Is Still Being Written
The Story of Three Chinese-Cuban Generals in the Cuban Revolution
Armando Choy, Gustavo Chui, and Moisés Sío Wong talk about the historic place of Chinese immigration to Cuba, as well as more than five decades of revolutionary action and internationalism, from Cuba to Angola and Venezuela today. Through their stories we see how millions of ordinary men and women opened the door to socialist revolution in the Americas, changed the course of history, and became different human beings in the process. $20. Also in Spanish and Chinese.

Pombo: A Man of Che's *guerrilla*
With Che Guevara in Bolivia, 1966–68
Harry Villegas
A firsthand account of the 1966–68 revolutionary campaign in Bolivia led by Ernesto Che Guevara. Under the nom de guerre Pombo, Harry Villegas, in his 20s at the time, was a member of Guevara's general staff. Villegas led the small group of combatants who survived the Bolivian army's encirclement and lived to recount this epic chapter in the history of the Americas. $23

Dynamics of the Cuban Revolution
A Marxist Appreciation
Joseph Hansen
How did the Cuban Revolution unfold? Why does it represent an "unbearable challenge" to U.S. imperialism? What political obstacles has it overcome? Written as the revolution advanced from its earliest days. $25

October 1962
The 'Missile' Crisis as Seen from Cuba
Tomás Diez Acosta
In October 1962 Washington pushed the world to the edge of nuclear war. Here the full story of that historic moment is told from the perspective of the Cuban people, whose determination to defend their sovereignty and their socialist revolution blocked U.S. plans for a devastating military assault. $25

www.pathfinderpress.com

Cuba & Africa

HOW FAR WE SLAVES HAVE COME!
South Africa and Cuba in Today's World
NELSON MANDELA, FIDEL CASTRO
Speaking together in Cuba in 1991, Mandela and Castro discuss the place in the history of Africa of Cuba and Angola's victory over the invading US-backed South African army, and the resulting acceleration of the fight to bring down the racist apartheid system. $10. Also in Spanish.

CUBA'S INTERNATIONALIST FOREIGN POLICY
FIDEL CASTRO
The revolutionary leader's speeches on solidarity with Angola, Ethiopia, Vietnam, and Nicaragua, including "Angola: African Girón" (1976). Also includes "Cuba in Angola: Operation Carlota" by Gabriel García Márquez (1977). $22

FROM THE ESCAMBRAY TO THE CONGO
In the Whirlwind of the Cuban Revolution
VÍCTOR DREKE
A leading participant in Cuba's revolutionary movement for more than half a century describes his experiences as second-in-command in the 1965 internationalist mission in Congo led by Che Guevara. Dreke also recounts his participation in the 1956–58 revolutionary war that toppled the US-backed Batista tyranny, as well as his command of volunteer battalions that defeated rightist bands after the revolution's triumph. $17. Also in Spanish.

IN DEFENSE OF SOCIALISM
Four speeches on the 30th anniversary of the Cuban revolution, 1988–89
FIDEL CASTRO
Castro describes the decisive place of volunteer Cuban fighters in the final stage of the war in Angola against invading forces of South Africa's apartheid regime. Economic and social progress, the Cuban leader says, is not only possible without capitalism's dog-eat-dog competition, but socialism is humanity's only way forward. Introduction by Mary-Alice Waters. $15

www.pathfinderpress.com

EXPAND *your Revolutionary Library*

The Working Class and the Transformation of Learning
The Fraud of Education Reform under Capitalism
JACK BARNES

"Until society is reorganized so that education is a human activity from the time we are very young until the time we die, there will be no education worthy of working, creating humanity." $3. Also in Spanish, French, Swedish, Icelandic, Farsi, and Greek.

We Are Heirs of the World's Revolutions
Speeches from the Burkina Faso Revolution 1983-87
THOMAS SANKARA

How peasants and workers in this West African country established a popular revolutionary government and began to fight hunger, illiteracy and economic backwardness imposed by imperialist domination, and the oppression of women inherited from class society. They set an example not only for workers and small farmers in Africa, but those the world over. $10. Also in Spanish and French.

Problems of Women's Liberation
EVELYN REED

Six articles explore the social and economic roots of women's oppression from prehistoric society to modern capitalism and point the road forward to emancipation. $15

www.pathfinderpress.com

Malcolm X Talks to Young People

"You're living at a time of revolution," Malcolm told young people in the United Kingdom in December 1964. "And I for one will join in with anyone, I don't care what color you are, as long as you want to change the miserable condition that exists on this earth." Four talks and an interview given to young people in Ghana, the UK, and the United States in the last months of Malcolm's life. $15. Also in Spanish.

Capitalism and the Transformation of Africa
Reports from Equatorial Guinea
MARY-ALICE WATERS, MARTÍN KOPPEL

An account of the transformation of class relations in this central African country, as it is drawn deeper into the world market and both a capitalist class and modern proletariat are born. The example of Cuba's socialist revolution comes alive in the collaboration of Cuban volunteer medical brigades there. Woven together, the outlines of a future to be fought for today can be seen—a future in which Africa's toilers have more weight in world politics than ever before. $10. Also in Spanish.

The Jewish Question
A Marxist Interpretation
ABRAM LEON

Traces the historical rationalizations of anti-Semitism to the fact that, in the centuries preceding the domination of industrial capitalism, Jews emerged as a "people-class" of merchants, moneylenders, and traders. Leon explains why the propertied rulers incite renewed Jew-hatred in the epoch of capitalism's decline. $22

www.pathfinderpress.com

Puerto Rico: Independence Is a Necessity
RAFAEL CANCEL MIRANDA

One of the five Puerto Rican Nationalists imprisoned by Washington for more than 25 years until 1979 speaks out on the brutal reality of U.S. colonial domination, the campaign to free Puerto Rican political prisoners, the example of Cuba's socialist revolution, and the ongoing struggle for independence. $6. Also in Spanish.

Black Music, White Business
Illuminating the History and Political Economy of Jazz
FRANK KOFSKY

Probes the economic and social conflicts between the artistry of Black musicians and the control by largely white-owned businesses of jazz distribution—the recording companies, booking agencies, festivals, clubs, and magazines. $17

Understanding History
Marxist Essays
GEORGE NOVACK

How did capitalism arise? Why and when did this exploitative system exhaust its potential to advance civilization? Why revolutionary change is fundamental to human progress. $20

www.pathfinderpress.com

From the dictatorship of capital...

The Communist Manifesto
Karl Marx, Frederick Engels

Founding document of the modern revolutionary workers movement, published in 1848. Why communism is not a set of preconceived principles but the line of march of the working class toward power—a line of march "springing from an existing class struggle, a historical movement going on under our very eyes." $5. Also in Spanish, French, and Arabic.

State and Revolution
V.I. Lenin

"The relation of the socialist proletarian revolution to the state is acquiring not only practical political importance," wrote V.I. Lenin in this booklet just months before the October 1917 Russian Revolution. It also addresses the "most urgent problem of the day: explaining to the masses what they will have to do to free themselves from capitalist tyranny." In *Essential Works of Lenin*. $12.95

Their Trotsky and Ours
Jack Barnes

To lead the working class in a successful revolution, a mass proletarian party is needed whose cadres, well beforehand, have absorbed a world communist program, are proletarian in life and work, derive deep satisfaction from doing politics, and have forged a leadership with an acute sense of what to do next. This book is about building such a party. $16. Also in Spanish and French.

www.pathfinderpress.com

...to the dictatorship of the proletariat

Lenin's Final Fight
Speeches and Writings, 1922–23
V.I. Lenin

In 1922 and 1923, V.I. Lenin, central leader of the world's first socialist revolution, waged what was to be his last political battle. At stake was whether that revolution would remain on the proletarian course that had brought workers and peasants to power in October 1917—and laid the foundations for a truly worldwide revolutionary movement of toilers organizing to emulate the Bolsheviks' example. $20. Also in Spanish.

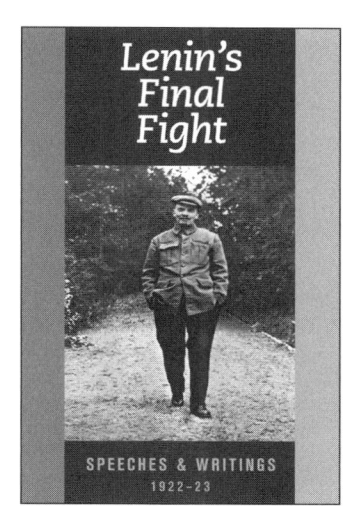

Trade Unions: Their Past, Present, and Future
Karl Marx

Apart from being instruments "required for guerrilla fights between capital and labor," the unions "must now act deliberately as organizing centers of the working class in the broad interest of its complete emancipation," through revolutionary political action. Drafted by Marx for the First International's founding congress in 1866, this resolution appears in *Trade Unions in the Epoch of Imperialist Decay* by Leon Trotsky. $16

The History of the Russian Revolution
Leon Trotsky

The social, economic, and political dynamics of the first socialist revolution as told by one of its central leaders. How, under Lenin's leadership, the Bolshevik Party led the overturn of the monarchist regime of the landlords and capitalists and brought to power a government of the workers and peasants. Unabridged, 3 vols. in one. $38. Also in Russian.

New International
A MAGAZINE OF MARXIST POLITICS AND THEORY

NEW INTERNATIONAL NO. 12
CAPITALISM'S LONG HOT WINTER HAS BEGUN
Jack Barnes
and "Their Transformation and Ours,"
Resolution of the Socialist Workers Party

Today's sharpening interimperialist conflicts are fueled both by the opening stages of what will be decades of economic, financial, and social convulsions and class battles, and by the most far-reaching shift in Washington's military policy and organization since the U.S. buildup toward World War II. Class-struggle-minded working people must face this historic turning point for imperialism, and draw satisfaction from being "in their face" as we chart a revolutionary course to confront it. $16

NEW INTERNATIONAL NO. 13
OUR POLITICS START WITH THE WORLD
Jack Barnes

The huge economic and cultural inequalities between imperialist and semicolonial countries, and among classes within almost every country, are produced, reproduced, and accentuated by the workings of capitalism. For vanguard workers to build parties able to lead a successful revolutionary struggle for power in our own countries, says Jack Barnes in the lead article, our activity must be guided by a strategy to close this gap.

Also in No. 13: "Farming, Science, and the Working Classes" *by Steve Clark.* $14

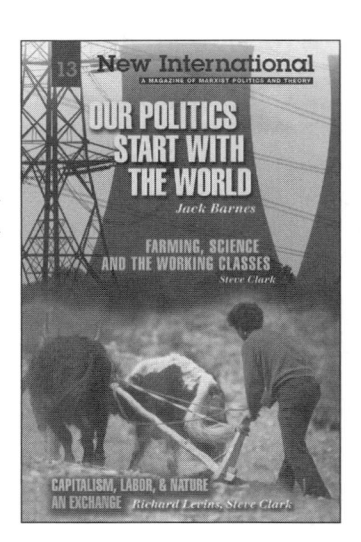

THESE ISSUES ARE ALSO AVAILABLE IN SPANISH AND MOST IN FRENCH AND SWEDISH AT
WWW.PATHFINDERPRESS.COM

NEW INTERNATIONAL NO. 11
U.S. Imperialism Has Lost the Cold War
Jack Barnes

Contrary to imperialist expectations in the 1990s in the wake of the collapse of regimes across Eastern Europe and the USSR claiming to be communist, the workers and farmers there have not been crushed. The toilers remain an intractable obstacle to imperialism's advance, one the exploiters will have to confront in class battles and war. $16

NEW INTERNATIONAL NO. 8
Che Guevara, Cuba, and the Road to Socialism
Articles by Ernesto Che Guevara, Carlos Rafael Rodríguez, Carlos Tablada, Mary-Alice Waters, and Steve Clark and Jack Barnes

Exchanges from the opening years of the Cuban Revolution and today on the political perspectives defended by Guevara as he helped lead working people to advance the transformation of economic and social relations in Cuba. $10

IN NEW INTERNATIONAL NO. 10
Defending Cuba, Defending Cuba's Socialist Revolution
Mary-Alice Waters

In face of the greatest economic difficulties in the history of the revolution in the 1990s, Cuba's workers and farmers defended their political power, their independence and sovereignty, and the historic course they set out on at the opening of the 1960s. $16

PATHFINDER AROUND THE WORLD

Visit our website for a complete list of titles and to place orders

www.pathfinderpress.com

PATHFINDER DISTRIBUTORS

UNITED STATES
(and Caribbean, Latin America, and East Asia)
Pathfinder Books, 306 W. 37th St., 10th Floor,
New York, NY 10018

CANADA
Pathfinder Books, 7107 St. Denis, Suite 204,
Montreal, QC H2S 2S5

UNITED KINGDOM
(and Europe, Africa, Middle East, and South Asia)
Pathfinder Books, First Floor, 120 Bethnal Green Road
(entrance in Brick Lane), London E2 6DG

AUSTRALIA
(and Southeast Asia and the Pacific)
Pathfinder, Level 1, 3/281-287 Beamish St., Campsie, NSW 2194
Postal address: P.O. Box 164, Campsie, NSW 2194

NEW ZEALAND
Pathfinder, 4/125 Grafton Road, Grafton, Auckland
Postal address: P.O. Box 3025, Auckland 1140

Join the Pathfinder Readers Club
to get 15% discounts on all Pathfinder titles
and bigger discounts on special offers.
Sign up at www.pathfinderpress.com
or through the distributors above.